IOS 12/15

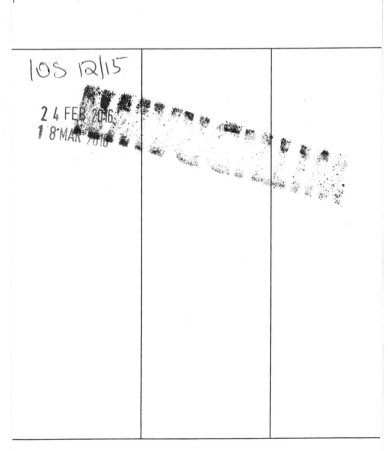

AN ENGLISH SPRING

AN ENGLISH SPRING

Memoirs

CORMAC MURPHY-O'CONNOR

BLOOMSBURY

LONDON • NEW DELHI • NEW YORK • SYDNEY

Bloomsbury Continuum

An imprint of Bloomsbury Publishing Plc

50 Bedford Square	1385 Broadway
London	New York
WC1B 3DP	NY 10018
UK	USA

www.bloomsbury.com

Bloomsbury, Continuum and the Diana logo are trademarks of Bloomsbury Publishing Plc

First published 2015

British Library Cataloguing-in-Publication Data
A catalogue record for this book is available from the British Library.

ISBN: HB: 9781472913142
ePub: 9781472913159
ePDF: 9781472913166

10 9 8 7 6 5 4 3 2 1

Typeset by Fakenham Prepress Solutions, Fakenham, Norfolk NR21 8NN
Printed and bound in Great Britain by CPI Group (UK) Ltd, Croydon CR0 4YY

To find out more about our authors and books visit www.bloomsbury.com. Here you will find extracts, author interviews, details of forthcoming events and the option to sign up for our newsletters.

CONTENTS

LIST OF ILLUSTRATIONS

First plate section

1. Grandfather Murphy-O'Connor and family. Cork, 1920.
2. The Murphy-O'Connor family.
3. The Murphy-O'Connor family home. Reading, 1947.
4. The English College rugby team. Rome, 1951.
5. Day of our audience with Pope Pius XII. Rome, 1951.
6. Cardinal Griffin, staff and students of the English College. Rome, 1950.
7. Ordination as Bishop of Arundel and Brighton, 1977.
8. Meeting Pope Paul VI after being appointed Bishop of Arundel and Brighton. Rome, 1977.
9. Working as secretary to Bishop Derek Worlock.
10. With Cardinal Basil Hume after being ordained as Bishop of Arundel and Brighton, 1977.
11. Meeting my young namesake after being ordained Bishop at Arundel cathedral, 1977.
12. Being created cardinal by Pope John Paul II. Rome, 2001.
13. In conversation with Pope Benedict XVI.
14. A meeting of Pope Benedict and the secretariat of the synod of bishops.
15. In friendly conversation with the Archbishop of Canterbury, Rowan Williams.
16. On the golf course with Fr Edward Corbould and Archbishop Michael Bowen.
17. With Professor Henry Chadwick, a fellow member of ARCIC.

Introduction

An uncertain time

When I was installed as Archbishop of Westminster on 22 March 2000 I mentioned a stone I had come across on a small island in the Outer Hebrides. On it was inscribed, *Pilgrim Cormac,* and, below, were the words, *He went beyond what was deemed possible.* There were ripples of amusement among the congregation inside the cathedral. As I reminded them, before my appointment the bookmakers had me listed as a 25-to-1 outsider.

Now that I have been in retirement for a number of years, there has been a certain pressure on me to write an account of my life. This has not only come from others, but from my inner self. I am the only Archbishop of Westminster to have retired; all of my nine predecessors died in office. With the exception of the great Cardinal Manning, who lived until he was 86 years old, they all died before they reached the age of 80. The only one of my predecessors who attempted an autobiography was Cardinal John Carmel Heenan. He completed two volumes, but the record of his personal story ceased at the point he became Archbishop of Westminster. I am the only one to have had a little time to reflect back on my life and to try to put into perspective some of the things that have touched me during my life as priest, bishop and cardinal.

I suppose the most difficult thing about writing an account of one's life is to express something of the 'inner me', the 'real Cormac'. It is easy enough to set down the various events that have occurred during one's life, but to try to put into words the emotions that underpinned them is more difficult. It is harder still to talk honestly about the sorrows and conflicts we have faced, the hurts we have caused, the mistakes we have made. Many of my experiences are common to the life of every priest. How have I tried to relate my faith to my life? How have I tried to live as a human being, with all its inevitable successes and failures, aspirations and hopes? How have I been able to give and receive love and affection, without which life would be unbearable?

I had the great blessing of being brought up in a secure and loving family. I had an uncle who was a priest and who used often to give a little speech at family gatherings in which he would quote the words of Isaiah: 'Remember the rock out of which you were hewn.' By 'rock' he meant the rock of family and the rock of faith. Certainly, to be brought up as I was in a large and loving family has been the foundation of my life. This is why I have always been deeply concerned about family life and its stability. There is plenty of research to support the belief not only that marriage provides the greatest possibility of stability for children, but that the love and commitment of a happy marriage is itself the best foundation upon which children can build lasting relationships in their own lives. All this I learnt not only from the experience of my own family, but from my participation and the part I have played in so many marriages, through good times and bad.

Faith has been my other rock. The Catholic Church has always been the centre of my life. When Jesus left us to return to his Father he promised that he would not leave us orphans, he would come back to us, and therefore he has left us his Holy Spirit and his Church. I have always understood that since Jesus came to live among us, we are no longer alone, that the world is no longer without a heart. It is the Holy Spirit who enables us to confront the trials of the world and to be a disciple of the gospel of Jesus Christ. The Church, as Hugo Rahner (brother of Karl) said, is 'the Mary of the history of the world'. So the Church has always been my heart and my home. It has brought order to my life, a sense of beauty, and a sense of belonging to a living tradition that has been handed down through the centuries. I understand better than most the weakness of the Church and, of course, I know only too well the sinfulness, sometimes grave, of its members, yet it has always been and remains the centre of my faith and my prayer.

The Church I was brought up in was in a way a kind of fortress. In the picture we were given, there was One Church in which was brought forth the fullness of truth and life. This was found in the prayer of the faithful, in the sacraments and in the unity and strength that came from belonging to a universal Church. There were few signs of what you might call an ecumenical spirit, nor was there a real opening to the riches of the Bible or a fruitful appreciation of the Church's mission to be a sign and servant of the modern world.

When I was studying for the priesthood, my teachers spoke of the Councils of the Church and of the truths of the revelation of Jesus Christ, but they seemed to concentrate more on prohibitions, on dire warnings, sinful practices and false teaching. Then came Pope John XXIII and his bravery and trust in God in calling the second Vatican Council, which dramatically changed the face of the Catholic Church. No longer a closed fortress, it was now encouraged to be open to fellow Christians, to people of other religions and to the modern world. We were invited to become a Church that saw herself first of all as the pilgrim People of God, and every one of us, lay person, priest or religious, was called, to holiness.

At the end of the Council I was fortunate to work closely with the newly ordained bishop, Derek Worlock, who was enthusiastic to communicate the insights of the Council in every possible way. Lay people were encouraged to play their part fully in the life of the Church. There was the beginning of a real openness and friendship with fellow Christians. And we began to understand the Church, not so much as above the world, as 'the city on the hill', but within the world, as the leaven in the mass. In the years that followed I became the rector of a seminary in Rome and I had to learn how to form future priests – not an easy task in the new circumstances in which they would have to live. And then for many years I was a bishop, twenty-three of them in the diocese of Arundel and Brighton and nine in the archdiocese of Westminster.

Although I recall the events of my life, and, especially, the people I have met and the challenges I have faced, my account is coloured by my vision of the Church and its mission in today's world and by my understanding of the way the Church has developed, especially in England and Wales, during the past forty years. So this is more than just one man's life story. It is also a personal reflection on the way in which the Holy Spirit has guided the Church during the past fifty years. It is a story of one man's pilgrimage as priest, bishop and servant of God's Church, a story of faith and life, and a story of the Church in the world.

Cardinal Heenan called the first volume of his autobiography *Not the Whole Truth*, because, of course, it couldn't be. Many of the people he wrote about were still alive, and charity or prudence made full disclosure impossible. This memoir is not the whole truth either, though I have tried to be as open and honest as I can be. I hope you will forgive me for the informality of Christian names or short forms; 'Basil' and 'Derek' and so on is how I knew them, and it would seem artificial in a personal memoir to set out their full title at every mention. And I hope historians will forgive me for not trying to recount the details of every appointment, dispute or difficult decision. This is not intended to be a scholarly account of my time as a bishop and archbishop, but a personal record of some of the more interesting or significant personalities, events and ideas that have shaped my life. As Voltaire said, 'If you want to bore the reader, tell him everything'.

There are many people who have helped and encouraged me in the writing of this book, and who have commented on the text, helping to fill in the gaps in my memory and preventing some – though I fear not all – errors and omissions: for those that remain, I take full responsibility. In particular, Sr Damian McGrath prepared the original typescript and has read and reviewed every revision since. I also wish to thank Brendan Walsh, with whom I have spent many enjoyable hours discussing the format and content of this memoir. Without his help it may never have been completed.

In trying to think of a title, I turned to the famous sermon John Henry Newman gave to the English Catholic bishops in July 1852 at St Mary's, Oscott, Birmingham. They were meeting in Synod for the first time since the restoration of the hierarchy in 1850, the first time that Catholic bishops had formally gathered together in England since the Reformation. It was an emotional occasion, with the preacher and most of his hearers in tears as Newman recalled the penal times when Catholics in England had been persecuted and reduced to a despised remnant, and spoke of his hopes for a renewal, 'a second Spring'. Then he went on to say: 'Have we any right to take it strange, if, in this English land, the spring-time of the Church should turn out to be an English spring, an uncertain, anxious time of hope and fear, of joy and suffering,—of bright promise and budding hopes, yet withal, of keen blasts, and cold showers, and sudden storms?'

Aren't English springs always full of promise, and always marred by cold and grey and rain? And yet isn't the rain also a promise of crops to come, of labour not in vain? The pattern of my life, like that of the Church in recent years, has been an uncertain time of hopes and joys, of fears and of 'keen blasts'. It's been something of an English Spring.

1

The youngest son

Twelve days before he died on 17 June 1999, I went to visit Cardinal Basil Hume at the Hospital of St John & St Elizabeth in St John's Wood. When I entered his room, the first thing Basil said to me was: 'Cormac, you will have to take over this job.'

Was he just saying this as a friend paying me a compliment, or did he really know who his successor would be as Archbishop of Westminster? I was thrown. He seemed to speak with such assurance and I wondered how he could have known the mind of Pope John Paul II. Of course, even then I could not be certain if I would be asked to take over, and in fact the appointment was not confirmed until the following February. But Basil's words certainly gave me pause for thought. We went on to speak for ten minutes or so about church affairs and although by that time he was rambling a little, he was perfectly coherent. For me, it was good to see him for the last time; he was a man for whom I had the greatest admiration. At the end, we prayed together and blessed each other. I left the room, never to see him again.

On my way home I could not help thinking of the responsibilities that might lie ahead. The thought of being Archbishop of Westminster filled me with apprehension – and some excitement. And it made me think of my own life and background and the family that had nourished me.

I was fortunate that at the age of seven, when the Second World War broke out, my parents arranged for me to stay with relations over in Cork, because they thought Reading was going to be bombed to bits. I was left with my father's parents.

The Murphy-O'Connors were not rich but they had, as they say in Ireland, 'the name of money'. When I lived with my grandparents it was not in the house my father had grown up in – that overlooked the estuary – but in a lovely rambling house on the banks of the river Lee. I'm often asked how the name 'Murphy-O'Connor' came about. There are plenty of Murphys in the world and plenty of O'Connors but not so many Murphy-O'Connors. The story goes that in the early part of the nineteenth century a Mary McSweeney married a Michael Murphy. They had children; then Mr Murphy died, and the widow remarried, this time to a Mr O'Connor, and there were further children. So the Murphys and the O'Connors grew up together. One of the Murphy boys, Daniel, became a priest and volunteered for the missions. He was sent to Hyderabad. Within a few years, his bishop asked Rome for Daniel to be appointed his coadjutor. He was consecrated in Kinsale, where his brother Denis was the parish priest, in 1846. He was 36 – the youngest bishop in Christendom at the time. After twenty-five years in India his health broke down and he returned to Ireland, but within a few months he had recovered and he was appointed bishop of Hobart, Tasmania. He took his nephew with him, and was soon followed by another nephew and by his sister and four other nuns from Fermoy, who opened the first Presentation convent and school in the southern hemisphere. Bishop Murphy attended the first Vatican Council in 1869, and voted for papal infallibility. He remained in Hobart as bishop for thirty-six years. The Holy See gave him the title of Archbishop late in life, perhaps in the hope that he might get the message and resign. He didn't. He died at the age of 96, still in office, one of the oldest Catholic prelates in the world.

Of the other Murphy and O'Connor children, it seems that two of the brothers set up a wine importing business. I remember travelling up the Cork estuary with my father and him pointing out to me a warehouse at the side of the river. On it was written, rather quaintly, 'Murphy and O'Connor Brothers, Dispensers of Wine and Spirits to the Clergy and Gentry of Southern Ireland'. My grandfather took over the business and the name, calling himself 'Murphy-O'Connor'. He went all around the presbyteries and grand houses of Cork and Kerry plying the 'clergy and gentry' with his wines and spirits. In those days, the railway system in Ireland was very extensive, much like it was in England before Mr Beeching rationalized it. Normally, my grandfather would travel by train, which would stop at tiny stations dotted all over Cork and Kerry at the request of the great land-owners. My grandfather would ring the station master at Killarney or Limerick to tell him that the Lord of the Manor wanted the train to stop at such-and-such a place, which accordingly it did. My grandfather would be the only person alighting from the train, and after concluding his business he would return to the station, where he would be the sole passenger picked up by the train on its return journey to Cork.

I know little about my grandfather's first wife because, tragically, she drowned on their honeymoon. There is a Murphy-O'Connor tomb in my cousin Kerry's parish in Turner's Cross, Cork, where she is buried. She was not mentioned very much. Fairly soon afterwards, my grandfather married Margaret Courtney from Fossa, near Killarney, and naturally enough she did not want to talk about his first wife.

My grandparents had nine children, seven boys and two girls. My father, Patrick George, was the eldest and was always called 'George', as he was born on St George's feast day. He was followed by Kerry, who took over the business; my uncle Jim, who also became a doctor and later joined my father as his partner in the practice in Reading; then Arthur ('Artie'), who became a priest; John, the third brother to become a doctor; and then there were the two younger ones, Joe and Donal, who also became priests. So there were three priests, three doctors and the businessman. One of the daughters, Kathleen, married a prominent Cork businessman called O'Shea, and and the other, Emma, became a nun in Drishane, at the convent of the Holy Infant Jesus. She stayed there all her life. She was a wonderful person, a very talented artist and, even though she wore this great habit, she was a free woman and the girls loved her – a lot of them joined the Order because of her.

My grandmother was teasingly known in the family as 'the Queen of Fossa'. She used to call my grandfather 'the Boss' – because of course he wasn't. I was very fond of my grandfather. He always used to go out wearing a hat and carrying a walking stick, and he had his own special chair in the house which only he was permitted to sit on. I remembered him many years later when I preached at a celebration in the cathedral in Cork. Just like a bishop, my grandfather had his hat, his stick, and his own special chair.

The Murphy-O'Connor family seems to have been very well known in Cork. My father and his six brothers were for one year all together at the Christian Brothers' School. They were prominent in all sports, but particularly rugby. After he left school George went on to study medicine at University College Cork. I sometimes wonder if he ever thought of the priesthood – I don't know. He was the captain of the rugby team and, a little later, captain of Munster. Why, after qualifying as a doctor, did my father leave Cork? He would have fairly easily have obtained a practice in Cork or Kerry. Perhaps there was something in him that wanted to get away from the rather narrow atmosphere of a small city, where everybody knew everybody else. And he may have had the urge to travel too. It's an Irish thing. Many Irish doctors and dentists followed the Irish missionaries and other emigrants who went abroad in their thousands to England, America, Australia and elsewhere.

George settled first in St Helens, where he became a junior doctor in a large practice. Being an Irish citizen he was not called up during the First World War and he remained in the north of England until, in 1918, he had saved up enough money to secure a practice in Reading. The first years were difficult. The practice had been allowed to run down and it was very hard work building it up again. After a few years, George was joined by his younger brother, my uncle Jim. When he reached the age of 32 the Bishop of Portsmouth, William Cotter, who was a friend, suggested to George that it might be time to 'settle down'. There were a number of young women in Reading who might have considered my father a good catch, but he was friendly with a young woman in Cork and he decided that he would go over and see her and perhaps make an arrangement to marry. They agreed to meet in a little coastal village near Cork where they had often been on holidays, called Ballycotton. At the last moment, the young woman invited her best friend to accompany her on this fateful expedition. As so often in fiction, as well as in real life, my father fell in love with the best friend. Within a fortnight they were engaged and soon after were married by Bishop Cotter in the beautiful Honan Chapel at University College Cork.

My mother was Ellen Cuddigan. She came from Cloyne, a small village in Co. Cork, famous as the birthplace of the greatest hurler of all time, Christy Ring. There is now a statue of him in the village. The other famous person with Cloyne connections is George Berkeley, who was the Protestant Bishop of Cloyne in the eighteenth century. Berkeley is often regarded as the father of idealism, and the greatest bishop/ philosopher since St Augustine, though it has to be said that doesn't make him as famous as Christy Ring, at least in Cork. My brother Brian once managed to pass a philosophy exam at the Gregorian University in Rome on the strength of what he was able to tell the Professor about Bishop Berkeley. It was not so much his exposition of Berkeley's ideas but the fact that his mother had been born in Cloyne that impressed the examiner.

My grandmother on my mother's side was a widow by the time I knew her. The Cuddigans owned a shop, a pub and a farm, and her eldest son, James, as was customary, had taken over the farm and the butcher's shop. James was a remarkable man, the sage of the village, and although he was not able to have tertiary education himself, his grand-children and great-grandchildren became distinguished in many fields, both in Ireland and beyond. My mother, Ellen, and the other brother, John, went to University College Cork, my mother to study commerce and French and her brother to study medicine. After qualifying, John became a ship's doctor for a number of years and then settled into a good practice in Windsor.

Ellen was only 21 when she married George. It was quite an adventure for her to travel from Cloyne over to Reading and to begin a new life. George's home had been a doctor's house for over a hundred years. I remember every detail of it. It was a large house in the centre of Reading with twenty-one rooms, including seven bedrooms. We had four stables outside, once used for the horses, a garage that had been converted from the main stable, and a biggish garden at the back. The surgery was in the middle of the house with two doors. One door led to the panel patients' waiting room; panel patients had their doctor's fees paid by their employers. The other door led to the private patients' waiting room; they paid their doctor's fees from their own resources. The panel patients' room had *Picture Post* and the *Illustrated London News* on the table; the private patients had copies of the *Tatler* and *Country Life*. Outside the front door of the house there was a hole in the wall which was connected by a small pipe to the doctor's bedroom. In earlier times, a caller could blow into the hole during the night and the noise would wake the doctor up so that he could attend to his patient.

Before the war the house was a hive of activity, with patients calling and five boys running around. When I was young we had quite a Victorian household. We had two maids, and I'm told that before my time we even had a boot boy, who had to be let go when he outgrew his uniform! My mother didn't 'work'. But of course, running this household was a considerable task. We also had, rather surprisingly, a French governess. My mother wanted her boys to learn the language, so she decided that for one meal a day we would only be permitted to speak French. The governess and my mother would start a conversation and then we boys would be encouraged to keep it going. After a long silence, one of my older brothers would say, in a funny accent, '*voulez-vous me passer les pommes de terre*', and there would be laughter all round. Ellen did her best, but her attempt to produce five cultivated sons was not a great success.

My father gave us challenges, to collect wild flowers or to cultivate a little bit of the garden, and I became something of a gardener. He once issued a challenge to my three eldest brothers, then aged 13, 12 and 10, to go to Ireland, not in the usual way by train but by bicycle. He put them on the train at Reading and told them to get off at Bristol. There he had put in the Post Office a little money for them to collect and they were told to cycle on to Newport, Cardiff, Swansea and ultimately to

Fishguard, where they would catch the ferry over to Ireland. My father had deposited some money in the Post Office in each town along the way, so that they would have enough for each day. My mother was very worried at her young sons going off together and waited anxiously for some sign that they were safe. Eventually, a card came from Rosslare in Ireland with the laconic message: '*All sick. No money. Love, Jim.*'

Every year my father took a house in Ireland for the month of August. It was in a little seaside village called Ardmore in County Waterford. George and Ellen and a maid lived in the cottage and we five boys were put in what was called a 'dug-out', a shed where we all slept in bunks. Each morning before breakfast my father would shout for us to come and have a swim, which we did with great reluctance. Those holidays remain in my memory as days of swimming and boating and picnics. I remember particularly one picnic at a place called Goat Island. It was my fifth birthday and all the wider family had been invited to the party. As we all sat down and ate our picnic, one of my uncles said to me: 'Take off your cap and go round and say to everybody, "Sixpence for the birthday boy".' So immediately I went round holding out my cap, saying to everyone, 'Sixpence for the birthday boy'. I amassed a considerable amount of money. This was my first experience of something resembling the offertory collection.

All this changed with advent of war in 1939, when my parents decided to leave their five boys in Cork to be cared for by relatives. This was how, at the age of seven, I came to stay with my father's parents in their house on the side of the river Lee. I went to school with my brother Brian to the Presentation Brothers, while my other brothers, Jim, Pat and John, went to the Christian Brothers on the other side of Cork. We were only in Ireland for the 'phoney' war. Nothing was happening and my parents wanted their boys back again in England.

So in May 1940 I left my grandparents' home and returned to Reading along with my four brothers.

We were back for the start of the Battle of Britain. I remember sleeping in the cellar of our house which had been reinforced with special wood to hold it up if the bombs fell. But the bombers mostly flew over Reading and we only got about five bombs in the whole war. We did not go to Ireland again for some time. The next family holiday we went on was to a place called Peppard, near Henley, where we stayed on a farm. All I remember was the five of us pinching apples from an orchard nearby. Jim, the eldest, organized it. Pat and John climbed the trees. Brian was at the bottom, and I was on my little bike, going up and down, keeping watch. I am reminded of St Augustine, who recounts in his *Confessions* how as a boy he and a group of his friends shook a laden fruit tree and 'carried off a huge load of pears'. I don't think we repented of our misdeeds as much as Augustine did.

Then the next year we took a house in Westward Ho!, near Bideford in Devon. I remember a fellow on the beach showing us some card tricks and promising a pound to anyone who could solve one of them. So we went home and worked at it all day and finally we discovered how it was done, but of course by the time we went back to the beach the man had gone, so we never got the pound.

Like other mothers, I suppose the great challenge of the war for my mother was to adapt to the shortage of food. She had five hungry boys to feed and I can still recall the powdered egg, spam, tripe and meagre portions of meat and butter that were our staple diet during those years. Those were stressful years for families in Britain. They took a great toll on Ellen and, especially, on George, whose health began to deteriorate after the war. I remember listening in our sitting room one day to the wireless, and being touched deeply for the first time by a piece of poetry. It was Winston Churchill quoting Arthur Hugh Clough's poem, 'Say Not the Struggle Naught Prevaileth'. I have never forgotten the third verse:

For while the tired waves, vainly breaking,
    Seem here no painful inch to gain,
Far back, through creeks and inlets making,
    Comes silent, flooding in, the main.

By 1943 we were able to go on holiday to Ireland again. How good it was to stay with my grandmother in Cloyne and to rejoice in the eggs and butter and milk and beef and mutton – food the like of which I had not experienced for what seemed like an age. We never travelled to Ireland by car, always by train and ferry. I would go up with my mother to Holyhead to cross over to Dublin. We would spend the night in Dublin and then we got on the train. I had to help put the turf on to light the fire for the train to continue on the way to Cork. It was a marathon journey. On returning we used to bring back the world and all – as much as we could of food. We used to pay a bursar to get us through the Customs. He made a lot of money, that chap. His son became a priest.

I went to two schools in England. The first was Presentation College. This was a good school, run by an Order of Brothers whom my father had asked to establish a school in Reading, which had no Catholic school at that time. He had first asked the Christian Brothers to come and they couldn't or wouldn't, though all of us eventually went on to the Christian Brothers' school in Bath, Prior Park. In those days families were canvassed to send their boys to Catholic schools. In the south of England, there was Downside and Douai, two Benedictine boarding schools, and Beaumont, near Windsor, run by the Jesuits. My mother wanted us to go to Beaumont because she thought the Jesuits would provide a better education than the Christian Brothers' school at Prior Park. However, my father had given his word to the Christian Brothers, whom he had been educated by, that he would send his boys to them.

I arrived at Prior Park in 1945. The building is a beautiful Palladian mansion built in the eighteenth century as a country house on a hill overlooking the city of Bath, later bought by the Benedictine, Bishop Baines, who had an ambitious plan to create England's first Catholic university. It was quite a small school, maybe 250 boys. It had been bombed in the war. It was very Christian-Brotherish; tough going really. The food was grim. The winters of 1946 and 1947 were bitterly cold, and the snow and ice prevented us from playing games for several months. In my second year I got appendicitis and my father came down, wrapped me in hot water bottles and brought me to the hospital in Bristol. I didn't excel particularly at school. The teaching at Prior Park was good enough, at least until what was then called 'School Certificate and Matric'. But there were few really qualified staff to teach specialist subjects, and the two years leading up to the Higher School Certificate (now 'A' levels) were not especially productive.

My particular gift was music, especially the piano. I had first learnt to play when I was six. I was instructed by a wonderful teacher called Belinda Heather, who taught music at Reading University. She was a patient of my father's and she agreed to take me on as a pupil. I remember attending wartime concerts in Reading Town Hall performed by Myra Hess, Solomon, Louis Kentner, Moura Lympany and many others. It became an option for me to remain at Presentation College, so that I could continue my piano lessons with her. In some ways I regret not continuing my lessons with Belinda Heather; the teaching of music at Prior Park was not in the same league. Music has always played an important part in my life. It was a delight, many years later, to be a guest on *Desert Island Discs* and to choose my eight records. The castaway's favourite was 'Praise to the Holiest' from Edward Elgar's setting of Newman's poem, *The Dream of Gerontius*.

There was a touch of the Victorian parent about my father. He had his routine. He would be up early in the morning, out to Mass, come back, do his surgery at 9, go out to make his calls and then back to lunch. Once a week, he would play a round of golf with his brothers and his friends. He was always smartly turned out, in a suit and bow tie. He was pretty strict. He would pull apart my brothers when he caught them fighting among themselves but he never had any serious problems with discipline. He had a bottle of whisky in the house but he only drank it on one occasion that I remember. In Ireland, on holiday, after having a swim he would come out and he would have half a pint of pale ale and a whisky, but it was medicine more than drink. When we stayed in a hotel in Ardmore, Kelly's Hotel, on the first night he would always buy a drink for everybody in the bar. There is that rather bad tradition in Ireland – you have to do your round – and George never wanted to be thought of as mean.

It seemed to me that George and Ellen were very happy. I think my mother would have been more adventurous if she had had her way. When she married she had just finished university and was only 21. My father was 32 and just wanted to settle down. Ellen was an elegant woman. She always dressed beautifully, and had a certain style. She distributed 'visiting cards' to other ladies of the town. Once or twice a year she would ring her sister-in-law and they would arrange to meet up in London to go on a shopping expedition. They would go to Harrods and enjoy a *thé dansant* in a hotel. She really loved these days out.

My parents were both keen for the children to do well, but Ellen was more anxious that we would look and act the part. She was aghast when the two oldest boys first came back from Prior Park. All the fine manners she had taught them were gone. When later, as a young priest, I became Derek Worlock's secretary, she insisted on buying me a new pair of cuff-links and a proper morning coat.

George joined her on one of her shopping trips to London once, but he never did it again. Occasionally they would go to a show, but by the time I was born my father had become more sedate. I think they did a bit of entertaining at home, but by the time I was around there wasn't much of it. They used to play bridge with friends; so it was bridge and golf, the family, the church, the practice – that was their life really. Because he was a doctor, my father had a car – not so usual then – and we were always having to get out while a puncture was repaired. My father was still practising until about 1953. In his last years his heart began to fail, and, increasingly, my mother had to care for him. She learnt to drive. And in later years, she had to take over the practice accounts, because my father, generous to a fault, would fail to send bills to the private patients, who were supposed to pay, to make sure some money was coming in.

We played games of all kinds in our garden, whether it was football or touch rugby or cricket. I used to team up with my eldest brother, Jim, who was always brilliant at rugby. I think we were a bit better than the other three. At Christmas time the two uncles and their families would come over. And we all had to do something. I played the piano and I remember my brother, John – a good mimic – would do impersonations. Then we would put on a concert and there would be funny sketches. Although we would sometimes bring friends home from school, we were very self-contained as a family, content with each others' company.

On the whole, my parents kept a lot to themselves and to their own people. George was once asked to be a Justice of the Peace in Reading, but he refused. He felt, I think, that his life was the family and the Church. Today it would be different. He would have integrated into society in the way that Catholics are more likely to do now. But he felt he was called to be faithful to his vocation as a father and as a doctor.

My father and occasionally my mother would be at weekday Mass at 7.30 in the morning, my father remaining for a quarter of an hour afterwards for his thanksgiving. Every night after evening surgery we all said the rosary. My father founded and was president of the Society of Vincent de Paul. There was an SVP in most parishes, in which men met together once a week to pray and to visit the poor of the district. It was practical Christian charity and it complemented my father's life and service to his patients. He was a sort of third curate in the parish really. My mother was president of the Union of Catholic Mothers. George and Ellen were in many ways the backbone of service in the parish in all kinds of ways.

My father was the official doctor for the Lourdes pilgrimage from 1920 to the early 1950s, when he stopped going. There was only one pilgrimage to Lourdes in those days, the National Pilgrimage. My mother went too, though not every year. My father used to come back exhausted. It was hard going, getting on the train at Victoria then travelling to the south of France by train through the night. One year he was at the hotel with Cardinal Bernard Griffin, who was Archbishop of Westminster between 1943 and 1956. My father used to tell Griffin old Irish stories and jokes, and he loved them. On this particular pilgrimage the cardinal was ill with heart failure and his own doctor had told him that on no account was he to go to the baths. It would kill him if he did, he insisted. My father, who must have had a drink,

said: 'Nonsense! Our Lady will look after you. Of course you must have
a bath.' The cardinal's secretary was Derek Worlock, and Derek gave
my father a look as much as to say, 'gosh, you are going to be out of
a job.' But Griffin was delighted, and the next day there was a solemn
procession through the town to the baths: the cardinal, Derek, the
cardinal's doctor, and my father, saying the rosary. The cardinal was
undressed and dipped into the baths. He survived, and my father was
applauded for his brave diagnosis.

Pope Paul VI called the Catholic home an *ecclesiola*, a 'little church',
because he believed the basic truths of faith and Christianity were
nurtured in a most crucial way in the home. That was certainly true of
the home in which I was brought up. It was taken for granted that there
was prayer every day and devotion to Our Blessed Lady, and regular
attendance at Mass, not only on Sundays but on some weekdays. To be
a Catholic was the most natural, familiar thing in the world. I lived, in
quite a deep way, the rhythms of Christian life. How well I remember
the preparations in Advent for Christmas and then the privations of
Lent, when as boys we would give up sweets and wait anxiously for the
drama of the last days of Our Lord's life, Holy Week; the delight of the
Mass on Holy Saturday evening and the end of Lent. 'Alleluia!' we used
to shout, and faith and life came happily together. Then in the time after
Easter there were the preparations for Pentecost and the coming of the
Holy Spirit, after which there were the joyous celebrations of Corpus
Christi and the Sacred Heart of Jesus. It all nourished a faith and piety
that formed and remained with me for the rest of my life.

My sister Catherine was born in 1942, ten years after me, and was
welcomed and loved in a special way. Sadly, she was born with a spinal
defect which increasingly affected her breathing. Catherine went to
school at St Mary's Ascot and then to Paris for a year before going on

to enjoy a successful career. Catherine was the life and soul of every party and a great boon for the family. I remember once the five of us holding her when she was a small child – I must have been about 11 – and tossing her from one to the other. My mother came out of the house and when she saw what we doing, she was horrified. But that was Catherine and her brothers: she was always in the arms of all of us. She died in 2006 at the age of 66 and was much mourned by everyone who knew her.

What happened to George and Ellen's other children? Their eldest son, Jim, studied medicine at St Mary's Hospital in London as well as the College of Surgeons in Dublin, and before he qualified he served in the Royal Navy for two years. He was a renowned rugby player and had a long career playing for different clubs and on one occasion played at Twickenham for Ireland. He and his wife Anne have six children and twenty grandchildren, all of whom are very dear to me. His youngest son, James, my nephew, is now headmaster of our old school at Prior Park, which is flourishing. The second son, John, went to Sandhurst after school and became a regular soldier serving in different capacities in stations in Hong Kong and Japan. He fought in the Korean War and was set for a good career in the Army. Very sadly, at the age of only 32, he contracted cancer and died within a few months, in 1960. It was a terrible shock, and an immense sorrow for all the family.

The other three sons, Pat, Brian and myself, all became priests. It may seem strange that so many of us were to follow the same vocation and I suppose some of this is partly due to the circumstances of our upbringing. I had uncles who were priests, one of whom, Donal, served in the Diocese of Portsmouth. Donal was a curate on Jersey when war broke out. It was a very difficult time for all the citizens of the Channel Islands and they were told by the Germans that they were in no way to contact anyone outside the Islands, and if they were caught listening to the wireless that they would be sent to prison or to a concentration camp. Donal went to his church and hid his wireless underneath some slabs of stone. Every night at 9 o'clock he and his fellow curate would lock the church, take out the wireless and listen to the news on the BBC.

I've sometimes missed not having a family of my own. It's just one of the things you sacrifice when you make a promise of celibacy. Jim used to bring girlfriends home, and we would all eagerly comment on them. I remember a particularly beautiful girl, an air hostess. One afternoon I saw the two of them together in the nursery. They were dancing to records. Of course there is sometimes a kind of loneliness. But I suppose it was natural for me to start thinking about the priesthood. Ellen was a little bit sorry, I think, because she had lost her boys for so long while they were growing up, away at school, or to stay in Ireland during the war, and then they had each left home. It was very hard on her to lose each of her five sons one by one; and I was the youngest. But there it was. At the age of 18, I left home to began my studies for the priesthood at the English College in Rome. The next stage of my life was about to begin.

2

La vita romana

I remember the actual occasion when I said for the first time that I wanted to be a priest. I was 15 and was home from school. I was in the car with my father, who was doing his rounds, visiting patients in the practice. He suddenly turned to me and said: 'Come on, now, Cormac. What about you? What are you going to do when you grow up?'

Immediately I said: 'I want to be a priest.'

It just came out quite spontaneously. It's the only moment I remember actually saying, 'I want to be a priest'. I don't remember being particularly aware that I had been thinking about the priesthood. It must have been on my mind, because I had wondered about becoming a doctor like my father, or even a musician. I enjoyed playing the piano and I was quite good in those days, although I don't think I could have made a career out of it. But none of the other professions had been in the family. Nowadays the children in the family are doing all sorts of things. But we were limited, in a sense, in choice.

Our home was always a place of hospitality for priests, who were always amply entertained by my mother and father. Curates always seemed to be dropping in, and visiting preachers would always be made welcome. I think the parish priest would tell them that they should go out for lunch, and they would find their way round to our house. The many visitors included Ronald Knox, who must have been giving a retreat in Reading, but I was away at school at the time so I missed the chance of meeting him. And of course, as well as the example of the Christian Brothers who had taught me at Prior Park, I had three uncles who were priests and two older brothers who were training for the priesthood in Rome. All of this, I am sure, had some part in making me reflect on the importance of priesthood. Priesthood was always there at the back of my mind.

In the long years since the day I told my father that I wanted to be a priest, amid all the ups and downs, I have never lost the conviction that it is what God wanted me to be. When I became rector of a seminary, I used to ask the students who wanted to come why they wanted to be a priest. Somehow, the best answers came from those who said that they weren't really quite sure but they just thought that maybe this is what God wanted them to do. I usually found that these young men had a genuine prayer life and were people who in some way were going out of their way to be of service to people in need.

Of course, it was the example of my mother and father that, more than anything, nourished my vocation to the priesthood. By the time I was 18 I had made up my mind and was ready for the next stage of my life. I decided that I wanted to apply for the Westminster diocese rather than my home diocese of Portsmouth. I thought London would be more exciting – the bright lights and the big city – and it wasn't too far from Reading. My father spoke to Cotter's successor as Bishop of Portsmouth, John King, but King would not agree to me going to Westminster. He said he wanted me to join my brothers at the English College in Rome, the 'Venerabile'. If he was presuming that the rector of the College would welcome a third Murphy-O'Connor he was mistaken. Two, it seemed, was quite enough. My brother Pat had to work hard to persuade the rector to take me. My father paid for the three of us. He was not a particularly well-off general practitioner but when he died, the Bishop said that he had been one of the diocese of Portsmouth's most generous benefactors.

The journey to Rome in October 1950 was my first time out of England, apart from trips to Ireland. Five of us travelled together on the train from London. Some were more smartly dressed than others. I was pretty casual, while one of us had come from a junior seminary and was kitted out in a black suit and tie. We must have looked an odd lot. Off we went across Europe. We slept in bunks, and had been given tickets for meals. I had my first taste of spaghetti on the train from Paris to Rome.

For a young man of 18 – still a boy, really – Rome seemed a wonderful, fabulously exciting city. I saw places I had only read or heard about – not only St Peter's but the Pantheon, the Forum, the catacombs and much else besides. It made a bit of a change after Reading. It was a Rome typified by films like *Three Coins in the Fountain* and *Roman Holiday*, which had Gregory Peck and Audrey Hepburn happily careering around the streets on a Vespa. It was also, of course, a Rome of extreme poverty, where most people were still struggling to make ends meet after the travails of the Second World War. In some ways, Italy was on the front line of the struggle between the democracies of the West and the encroaching communism of the Soviet bloc and Tito's Yugoslavia. Politics was dominated by the Christian Democrat Party, which had been founded and led by the great Alcide de Gasperi, and the Communist Party led by Palmiro Togliatti. The tussle for power between them was more social and tribal than ideological. Few Italians were really communists. They voted for the party because it promised them a better standard of living, just as other Italians voted for the Christian Democrats for the same reason.

It is a world that is well captured in the popular Don Camillo stories created by Giovannino Guareschi, set in a small town in the Po Valley in the years after the end of the war. The antagonism between the hot-headed parish priest, Don Camillo, and the obstreperous communist mayor Peppone symbolized the clash between two opposing cultures. Guareschi's stories reflected in a perceptive and good-natured way the mind and heart of the average Italian. Don Camillo and Peppone are two sides of the same coin. Behind the façade of hostility, each has a heart of gold, and each grudgingly admires the other. Fellow townspeople, they understand and respect the other. You might say, they needed one another. Often split when it came to a local affair, they were united in the face of outside adversaries.

The Church in Rome was in its heyday. Pius XII had proclaimed 1950 a 'Holy Year'. Pilgrims flocked to Rome from all over the world. For many of them, it was their first trip abroad, a sort of release after the austerities of the immediate post-war years, and a huge adventure. I remember one afternoon 500 excited pilgrims led by Cardinal Griffin, with his dynamic young personal secretary Derek Worlock, coming to tea at the College. Like the other new students, I went into retreat for a week and then we were more or less ignored while the other students were busy showing all these pilgrims around, returning to the College for supper with big tips in their pockets. Eventually, even the students who had only been Rome a few weeks had to be dragooned into showing pilgrims the city. I was allocated a busload to take care of, but of course I knew almost nothing about the city and its sights. I managed to get hold of a guide book, and while the pilgrims were getting out of the bus to look at a monument, I would dart around the corner ahead of them to mug up on the history of the place, which I would then recite with the aplomb of a seasoned Roman tour guide.

I was in St Peter's Square on the crowning moment of the year, when on 1 November the pope proclaimed the dogma of the Assumption of Our Lady into heaven at the end of her earthly life. It was much the biggest crowd I had ever seen. The pilgrims spilled out of St Peter's Square right down to the Tiber river. I was with a fellow student, Tony Kenny, who was a year above me. You could tell that Pius XII loved these huge gatherings. The Mass would take place in St Peter's Basilica, but you had to have a ticket to be allowed in, and of course Tony and I hadn't been sent invitations. We went round to a side entrance, brought some papers out of our pockets and brandished them at the Swiss guards on the doors, explaining that we were secretaries to two cardinals who were already inside. They let us in and we found ourselves two excellent seats. The size of the crowd, the extraordinary mix of people from all over the world who were there, lay people, young and old, priests and nuns, students and seminarians from the various colleges, created an impression that has never left me of the universality of the Church. It was a magnificent celebration which typified in many ways the life of the Catholic Church in the years before the second Vatican Council: a little too comfortable in its certainties, somewhat triumphalist and inward-looking, and firmly opposed to the decadence and 'world-liness' outside.

It's not easy to sum up 'pre-Vatican II Catholicism'. Every Catholic was expected to know his or her 'penny catechism'. There was fish on Friday (now restored), and fasting from midnight before receiving Holy Communion the next morning. There were popular devotions such as the Nine First Fridays. There was Eucharistic adoration outside Mass, the recitation of the rosary, the veneration of favourite saints and the wearing of scapulars. Above all, the Mass, the central act of the worship of the Church, was in Latin, with the priest with his back to the people. A sense of awe and mystery permeated its celebration. It is no wonder that some people, including Pope Emeritus Benedict, love this old liturgy and want to give people the opportunity to attend it.

But there was more to the Catholicism of the 1950s than this. In those days, 'mixed marriages' – in other words, marriages between a Catholic and a non-Catholic – were seriously frowned upon and common prayer and common witness with fellow Christians was not to be tolerated. I suppose also the 'world' was treated with suspicion. In England Catholics were still regarded as somewhat on the periphery of society, not expected to contribute in any significant way to the political or social life of the country. Notwithstanding the contribution of such notable Catholic writers as G. K. Chesterton, Hilaire Belloc and Ronald Knox and, later, Graham Greene and Evelyn Waugh, or the widespread admiration for Leonard Cheshire and his homes for disabled people, Catholics were largely resigned and, indeed, content to remain in a subculture of their own, fortified by mutual support and a common faith.

Rome, of course, was very different. The city and its inhabitants were proud of their lovely churches and the intimate connection between the Church and the world was exemplified by the thousands of clerical students, dressed in distinctive cassocks, who walked the streets and frequented the universities. I was to live in Rome for seven years. It became part of me. The *vita Romana* was to be written into my heart.

The English College is on the Via di Monserrato, in the heart of medieval Rome. At the end of the street is the Piazza Farnese, and beyond that the Campo dei Fiori. The flower sellers who had given the square its name hundreds of years previously still display their wares in a riot of colour and it is filled with the cries of stallholders imploring passers-by to try their artichokes and cauliflowers, melons and peaches.

The College is the oldest English institution in Europe. It had been founded in 1362 as a hospice for English pilgrims to Rome and this is what it remained until the Reformation.

From earliest times pilgrims had visited Rome and the foundation of the College had been a lay initiative, the work of a confraternity formed in the years following the Holy Year of 1350. The hospice had distinguished wardens such as Thomas Linacre, scholar and founder of the Royal College of Physicians, William Warham, future Archbishop of Canterbury, and John Colet, renaissance scholar and Dean of St Paul's. By the time of King Henry VII, the hospice was controlled by the Crown and the King personally appointed the warden. Henry VIII's breach with Rome marked a great falling off in the number of pilgrims and the last warden, Cardinal Reginald Pole, was appointed by the pope, to ensure that his first allegiance would be to the Papacy rather than to the English Crown. Pole later became the Archbishop of Canterbury for a brief period in the reign of Mary Tudor; they died on the same day, 17 November 1558. With the accession of Queen Elizabeth the royal connection was lost. Twenty years later, owing to the increasing number of young men who wished to become priests, the hospice became a seminary.

The students were required to take an oath pledging loyalty to the pope and to return to England after ordination and work there. Over the next eighty years, forty-four students of the College died for their faith. Detailed descriptions of their form of martyrdom by hanging, drawing and quartering were displayed on the walls of the College, as a reminder to the students of what they might have to endure when they too returned to England. There were eighty or so students when I was there, and we lived under the shadow of those portraits and inscriptions. We were still being prepared for 'the mish' – and the mission was still, 'Let's convert England'. It wasn't until the Council and the decree on ecumenism that we realized – I think it was something I had come to realize a bit earlier – that Christians had to come together.

There were eleven of us in my year. We came from every part of England and Wales. Five of us had come from junior seminaries, mostly Ushaw or Upholland; four had come from Oxford University, having done their National Service; and two of us, including me, had come from independent schools. Most of us were 18-year-olds and straight from school, but there were also what we described then as 'late vocations' – in other words, young men in their early twenties. The education given to the students who had come from the junior seminaries was generally excellent, and these students arrived in Rome already very well versed in Latin and Greek as well as English and History.

In some ways life at the Venerabile was not dissimilar to an Oxbridge college in an earlier era. There was a regular rhythm of prayer, study and recreation. We were woken up in the morning by a bell at half-past five. We each had our own room. We had a jug and a basin for washing and shaving in our room, and there were bathrooms at the end of the corridor. Servants would come round and fill the jugs with water. We didn't have showers, we had baths – once a week. It was pretty spartan. But most of us had been brought up in grim conditions.

The day began with a half-hour meditation followed by Mass, and then breakfast, a bread roll with a bit of butter and coffee. We walked to the Gregorian University – 'the Greg' – where we had four lectures of three-quarters of an hour or so, and then we would troop back to the college for lunch. But first, with our stomachs rumbling, we would offer up prayers for the conversion of England. After these 'starvation prayers' we would go into the refectory for pasta, a bit of meat and some fruit. After lunch the students would all go to the common room and sit around for a while together. It was the same after supper, except that we would be joined by the rector of the college and all the staff. In the afternoon we went out for a walk in what was called a camerata – a group of four, all dressed in our cassocks. The idea was you had to go out and see some place of interest, a church or monument. There were also places where we could go to have a 'fag'. We were allowed to smoke – the rector, Gerard Tickle, used to smoke like a chimney. Inside the college we were only allowed to smoke at certain times, so we would go somewhere out of the way.

Each student had a priest-confessor who was also their spiritual director. My confessor was William Heard, a noted canon lawyer who worked in the Roman Rota. A Scot, he had been at Fettes school in Edinburgh, where his father had been headmaster, and after studying Law at Oxford he had become a Catholic and gone on to study in Rome. After ordination Heard served as a curate in Bermondsey in south London, but then he was called back to Rome to work as a canon lawyer, eventually becoming the Dean of the Holy Roman Rota, the equivalent of Chief Justice. A couple of years after I left the College in 1957 Pope John XXIII made him a cardinal, and he participated in the conclave that elected Montini to the papacy as Paul VI in June 1963.

Heard would often moan about the state of the curia. 'Pope Pius would rather meet a football team than pay any attention to the curia' – that sort of thing. There's nothing new about exasperation among senior churchmen with the Roman curia. He was a good confessor. And after hearing my confession we would sit and chat for a while and then he would send me away with a book. He had quite a large library. He would make a little note of the book I had borrowed to make sure I would return it. He was the one who really introduced me to a wider sort of reading, not just spiritual books but history and literature. He gave me a book on his favourite cardinal, the shrewd and wily Ercole Consalvi. Consalvi was the consigliere who managed things for Pius VI and Pius VII while Napoleon was rampaging around Europe. There's a fine painting of him by Thomas Lawrence in the royal collection. He's the cardinal who is said to have responded to Napoleon's famous threat that he would destroy the Church with the observation, 'Well, if after 1800 years all the clergy have failed to destroy the Church, do you really think you'll be able to manage it?'

I can't say that I much enjoyed my studies at the Gregorian. I'd be in a lecture theatre with students from all over the world – there were about three or four thousand of us in total, and there might be anything from 200 to 600 or so at a lecture. There was little or no personal interaction between the professors and the students. We sat on desks and we took notes. Or we fell asleep. The lecturers, nearly all Jesuits, spoke rapidly in Latin. Because all I had was my 'veni, vidi, vici' learnt at school, I found the first years particularly difficult. The exams were all oral. I can still see this Jesuit grilling me in my first exam on metaphysics. He would rattle off a question and then look up and ask, 'Yes or No?'

I paused for a moment. '*Utique!*' (Yes!)

He shook his head. '*Non!*'

'*Bene.*'

The professors were very kind to English students. Some of the philosophy I enjoyed. But theology was very flat, and the study of scripture was pretty awful. We didn't have to sign our names in a register or anything like that, and sometimes – if I had any money – I would just slope off and have a coffee and a bun or something. I was usually hungry. The truth is, I would probably have been better off if I had had three years at an English university studying something completely different before going to Rome.

A student who belonged to the Greek Catholic rite asked me for advice one day. Greek Catholic seminarians were permitted to get married, but had to do so before they received the diaconate. I asked him if he had a girl he might wish to marry and he said 'Yes'. But as he went on to explain, 'If I marry this girl, although I could be an ordained priest, I could not go on to become a bishop'. He asked my opinion. 'A bird in the hand is worth two in the bush', I said. He married the girl.

After my first examination in philosophy, together with three other students, we did something that was forbidden by the rules. We slipped into a *latteria* near the Trevi fountain for a cup of coffee and cake. As we sat in a side room drinking our coffee, a distinguished-looking priest I didn't recognize came in and ordered an espresso. When he noticed us, he came over and greeted us in halting English and asked us where we were from. We said, innocently, that we were English students and had just come from our first exam. He said he worked in the curia and wanted to welcome us to Rome and hoped we would be very happy here. He told us his name: Monsignor Montini. I had never heard of Montini, but later when I told Heard that I had met this polished curial official with not-so-good English, he said, 'Montini? You've met the next pope.'

The lovely thing about Montini was that he did not rebuke us for breaking the rules, but rather wanted to make sure that his first words were words of welcome. I got to know him quite well later when I was Rector of the College and he was Pope Paul VI. He was always the same, a man of welcome, of great humanity, who guided the Church through many difficult years.

Pius XII was a curious mixture. He did some excellent things. But even as a student, beside the assurance and the confidence, I could feel an increasing sense of inertia in Rome. There were no new cardinals being created, new ideas were being dampened down, liturgical renewal was being suffocated. I remember the great German theologian, Karl Rahner, coming to the Greg to give a talk and hearing some whispering because he was thought to be 'dangerous'. Even I knew this was ridiculous. The great French theologian, Henri de Lubac, was also under a cloud. I remember seeing one of the lecturers, a wonderful professor whom I admired enormously, and who I knew was a holy man and a fine scholar, talking about de Lubac, and there were tears in his eyes. Something was wrong.

Overall, the English College was a very sane institution. Many of us played football and rugby and even cricket at the villa at Palazzola overlooking Lake Albano and opposite the Papal summer palace at Castel Gandolfo, where we would spend three months every summer. We would have concerts and reviews, with songs and sketches. I played the piano quite a lot, and we used to do Gilbert and Sullivan operas. Once when I was playing the piano there was a chap sitting beside me plying me with white wine. At the interval we went in to supper and we switched to red wine. By the time we returned, the fellow saw I was pretty groggy so he took me out and put my head under a cold tap. I started the second half with a crashing crescendo. It wasn't the best production we had put on. Students dressed up and played both male and female parts, to general amusement. Young seminarians from the American and the Scots colleges would come over to see us. Pope John came once and was a little shocked at these antics.

Some evenings students and staff would watch a film together. We had one of those projectors where you had to change reels, so we would have to stop about six times during each showing. One year, I had the job of looking at the films beforehand to see if there were any unsuitable bits which should be extracted. There was one film which had Brigitte

Bardot in the starring role. It began with quite a steamy scene, so I went to the vice-rector and said, 'I am not sure about this one'. 'We'd better take a look', he said. So the two of us sat through the film together. He decided we could safely be permitted to enjoy it uncut.

When my parents came out for my eldest brother's Pat's ordination in 1951 the family had an audience with the pope. There were five of us: my parents, George and Ellen, Pat, Brian and myself. We had some influence through the Christian Brothers who had a school in Rome and one of them got our tickets for the audience. We were with about three other groups, waiting to greet the Holy Father. To a young seminarian in his first year, he was, of course, an awesome figure. My father looked very distinguished and my mother was as elegant as ever, in black, and, of course, with a lace mantilla. My father never said a word. I think I did most of the talking. I told the pope that I was finding the Latin very difficult. He assured me, in very bad English, that it would get better.

Although there were three Murphy-O'Connor brothers at the College the first year I was there, I tried to avoid the other two as much as possible. I made good friends – Jack Kennedy, who became rector after me, was one of them – though 'particular friendships' were not encouraged, without anyone specifically telling us why. I got to know all the students in my year well. There was Jack Brewer, who became a good friend, Richard Incledon, John Short, John O'Connor and Peter McGuire. There were some who were bright and some who were extraordinarily bright. Tony Kenny was one of those. He was miles ahead of the rest of us, so much so that we began to think that we must be pretty dim. I passed my exams, but never with the '10 out of 10' which Tony got all the time. Tony later left the priesthood, eventually becoming Master of Balliol. We remained good friends.

The closest friend I had at the college was Billy Mason. His family and my family were friends. His father, like mine, was an Irish doctor, and Billy and his brother had both been at Prior Park. We used to play in the same rugby team at school. So when he came out to Rome we became very good friends. But Billy left the college after three years. He just felt the priesthood was not for him. Later, he settled down and married in Ireland and his brother became a doctor in Dublin. It was something that happened, that you had to be prepared for. During those years of training for the priesthood we all had time to think. After three years in Rome, I came back to England for three months' holiday. That was a crucial time to go over the questions we all asked ourselves: What about me? Is this the right life for me? Should I stay? Or should I leave?

Each year after Easter and in late August the students took brief holidays in other parts of Italy and Europe. Over the seven years I visited Florence, Assisi, Subiaco, Venice, the Isle of Ischia and many other places of great interest. We were obliged to continue wearing our cassocks during these *gitas* and the people we met were accustomed to this. Indeed, when we hitch-hiked, the distinctive uniform was an advantage as cars were more inclined to stop and give us a lift, with the drivers inquiring about our life and vice versa. I have particularly vivid memories of three such *gitas*.

One was a walking holiday in the Stubaital valley in Austria. Four of us stayed in a small village and the simple life of the people moved me greatly. It was permeated by traditional values of a strong family life with mutual support and a deeply Christian piety. It seemed natural to all the people of the village. Here there was mutual companionship and support, a modest but very attractive way of living. Forty years later, with my friend Christopher Lightbound, I made a return visit.

Much was for the better: health care, communication, education, travel services. But much had been lost in the intervening years: the strength of the family, the sense of community and the shared joy in practice of their faith. The world had moved on with all its loss and gain.

On another summer *gita* I went climbing in the Alps with three friends from the College, including Tony Kenny. I remember well the ascent of Monte Rosa, a snow climb from Italy to Switzerland – a marvellous experience. We then endeavoured to climb the rock face of the Rothorn. A lightning storm suddenly descended upon us; the guide got thoroughly alarmed, and told us to throw away our ice axes. With lightning striking the rocks where we were stranded, I have rarely, if ever, felt so frightened. It might well have been the end of me and Tony. Thus would the world have been deprived not only of a future cardinal but, rather more important, one of the best English philosophers of the past fifty years!

Memories of another *gita* were stirred at the last meeting I had with Pope John Paul II. It was in 2003, just two years before he died. He was wheeled in in a chair. I decided to speak in Italian as I knew it would be easier for him. I asked him when he was going to beatify Cardinal John Henry Newman. He told me that we needed a miracle. I explained that the English were not very good at miracles – we did not like to 'bully' God as the Italians did. He smiled, and then I told him that I had been to see Padre Pio when I was a student in Rome. His face lit up.

'Me, too', he said, 'I also went to see him in my student days.'

We then spoke a little about holiness, the desire of every Christian heart. I am glad that at the last meeting I had with that brave and faithful pope, we spoke of holiness, the holiness of Blessed John Henry Newman and of St Pio of Pietrelcina. Karol Wojtyla's visit to Padre Pio had been soon after the Second World War. My own visit to San

Giovanni Rotondo, the small town in Puglia where the Capuchin friar lived in his monastery, was in 1953. I stayed in a hostel with three other students in a room with four beds. We decided that we would try to go to confession to Padre Pio the next day. We had heard that if we left anything out he would know. So we had a nervous night preparing our confessions. We only had one small Italian–English dictionary between us, which was passed from bed to bed. The next morning we went to his Mass. He was only allowed to say Mass in a side chapel at about 5 o'clock in the morning. Amazingly, there were already about 150 people crowded into the tiny space round. As soon as he appeared, the women shouted, 'Santo! Santo!' He told them sharply to keep quiet and say their prayers. He was wearing mittens and when he unfolded his hands we could see the stigmata, the wounds that corresponded to those of the Lord's crucifixion. Just after the consecration he went into a sort of ecstasy for what seemed like a quarter of an hour, and then again after holy communion.

After Mass we prepared to go to confession and because we had our clerical gear on we thought we might be able to jump the queue, but the Italians were having none of it. The queue for confession was a mile long, but we were able at least to greet him and to shake his hand. I felt privileged to have met him. I knew he was a truly holy man and I was delighted when Pope John Paul canonized him in 2002.

Each one of these three holidays reminds me of matters that have been very close to my heart during my life. The sojourn in the little village in Austria recalls for me the basic simple things that make a proper community – namely, family and friends and the local community, which form mutual support. Prime ministers may talk about building the 'big society', but the big society is formed by the small society: families and local communities that know and support one another with common values and common aspirations. This is where the big society begins and ends.

The Alpine holiday reminds me that if we wish to influence others for good we should be able to take decisions that involve some risk. 'Carpe diem', said Horace, and each day we should try to 'let go' and seize the moment to serve others in some way. And my visit to San Giovanni Rotondo and encounter with Padre Pio, now St Pio of Pietrelcina, is a powerful reminder that to strive to be holy is a daily task. The French writer, François Mauriac, wrote once that 'the only sadness is not to be a saint'. Holiness is what we are called to, whoever we are or wherever we are. For we who are Christians, it means to strive to become more like Jesus Christ in word and deed, people of prayer and service to others.

Like all the students at the College, I looked forward to my ordination as a priest, the culmination of the long years of preparation, prayer and study. All the family came to Rome: my mother and father, my four brothers, and my sister Catherine, who was 13 and who had to be given special permission to travel by her school. Most of my year at the College were ordained priest on the same day. Two of us – Jack Brewer and John Short – had been ordained the previous summer at the Villa but the rest of us were ordained together on 28 October 1956, then the Feast of Christ the King, at the Latin-American church, now the site of a police station. The bishop who ordained us was Luigi Traglia. Later, he went on to be vicar general of Rome and, before his death, dean of the College of Cardinals.

My father was not well at the time and he didn't want to go trudging round Rome too much. I managed to persuade the rector to let me go with my family down to Sorrento on the Bay of Naples for the week after the ordination. We were the only ones staying in the hotel. The waiter did not know what to make of us – this extraordinary family with three priests. My eldest brother Jim was already qualified as a doctor. A couple of years earlier I had spent an afternoon desperately traipsing from bar to bar in Rome trying to find a radio broadcasting the BBC World Service commentary on the match from Twickenham. Jim had been making his debut for Ireland. It was well into the second half before I struck lucky. The commentator was recapping: 'England had led 6–3 at half-time but the Ireland pack had been struggling since debutant James Murphy-O'Connor, the goal-kicking lock from Bective Rangers, had been stretchered off at the end of the first half.' There were no replacements in those days, remember. Jim had been nobbled apparently. My heart sank. England eventually won 14–3. It was Jim's only cap. My brother John, who was stationed in Germany, only had a few days with us before he was recalled to his regiment; it was the time of the Suez crisis and the Hungarian uprising. It was to be the last time my family were all together. John and my father both died in 1960, John from cancer and my father from heart disease.

I stayed on at the College until the following summer to get my licence in theology. I returned to England in 1957 to my home diocese of Portsmouth to begin my ministry as a priest. It was a very different world, and I soon found that I had a lot to learn.

3

The young curate

What was my frame of mind when I returned to England from Rome, a young Catholic priest ready and eager to fulfil the mission for which he had been trained?

It is difficult to appreciate how I might have seen the mission of the priest in 1957 without understanding how Catholics had been brought up to see the history of England in the years since the Reformation. In one sense I was coming 'home'. But in another sense, we saw it as a home that had been wrenched away from us, and England was, in a way, a place where we didn't quite fit. We had been taught that there was one Church founded by Jesus Christ, with the successor of Peter, the pope, at its head. After a millennium as a Catholic country, there had been a break with Rome, and for 400 years the people of England had been separated from the one true Church. Our role was to pray and work for the conversion of England and Wales – in other words, for the return of non-Catholics to full communion with the Catholic Church. That all seemed logical enough to a young seminarian training in Rome. For seven years I had, after all, lived under the shadow of the portraits of martyrs that had hung on the walls of the College. Even though I realized that it was a tall order, the conversion of England was always there in my hopes and aspirations. More prosaically and realistically, I saw that my other role as a priest was to 'keep the faith' – to nourish the spiritual lives of the Catholic people and to try and bring back the lapsed to the practice of their faith.

Like most Catholics who had been brought up in the years before the second Vatican Council began in 1962, I belonged to a subculture that was to a significant extent outside the mainstream of social and political life in England. We were not allowed to forget the brave martyrs, men and women, who had sacrificed their lives in the century following the accession of Queen Elizabeth I because of their faithfulness to the Catholic Church. We would be reminded of the centuries during which our co-religionists were barely tolerated.

In the famous sermon from which I have drawn my title, 'The Second Spring', John Henry Newman spoke – perhaps a little melodramatically – of:

a few adherents of the Old Religion, moving silently and sorrowfully about, as memorials of what had been. 'The Roman Catholics';—not a sect, not even an interest, as men conceived of it,—not a body, however small, representative of the Great Communion abroad,—but a mere handful of individuals, who might be counted, like the pebbles and *detritus* of the great deluge, and who, forsooth, merely happened to retain a creed which, in its day indeed, was the profession of a Church. Here a set of poor Irishmen, coming and going at harvest time, or a colony of them lodged in a miserable quarter of the vast metropolis. There, perhaps an elderly person, seen walking in the streets, grave and solitary, and strange, though noble in bearing, and said to be of good family, and a 'Roman Catholic'. An old-fashioned house of gloomy appearance, closed in with high walls, with an iron gate, and yews, and the report attaching to it that 'Roman Catholics' lived there; but who they were, or what they did, or what was meant by calling them Roman Catholics, no one could tell;—though it had an unpleasant sound, and told of form and superstition.

So when the Catholic Church began to grow again in England and Wales in the nineteenth century, largely due to immigration from Ireland and other countries, it was natural that its leaders would focus their energies on the creation of a network of dioceses and parishes and in building schools and churches. The dream of 'the conversion of England' was not lost, but inevitably the real task in hand was to 'keep the faith' and to hold together the Catholic community, many of whose members were very poor.

My first appointment was as curate in Corpus Christi parish in the North End of Portsmouth, where I was to spend five years. I immediately came face to face with the realities of life for the great majority of working people in post-war 'austerity Britain'. Many, if not most, of the parishioners were working in the naval dockyard. The husbands would cycle down to work at the docks, and they might be bringing home £5 a week. There were also the many widows of the sailors who had died during the war, struggling to get by on a tiny pension. I was shocked by the overcrowding and the poor housing conditions. My heart went out to these families.

The parish community was self-contained and tight-knit, on the edge of the city's social life and conscious of not having much influence in local affairs. Catholics clung together. When we had jumble sales the queue would be very long and people would come in to grab whatever clothes they could. The Union of Catholic Mothers would have to fight them off. Things didn't get better until the late 1950s or early 60s, when we started to build churches again. Like many other parishes in those days, we had a football pool. It raised about £150 a week, eventually enough for the down payment on the building of a Catholic school.

I lived in the presbytery with the parish priest, an Irishman, Gerry Dwyer. He was a good man and kind to me but he wasn't overly energetic. We had a housekeeper who would cook for us. Father Dwyer used to say: 'Cormac, you can't do anything until you have eaten well.' I had my own tiny bed-sitting room. After about three months I was delighted when a parishioner left me her piano. Unfortunately, after hoisting up the piano with great difficulty to my room, I found, after a few weeks, that it had dry rot, and I had to get rid of it. I always wore my clerical collar and a black suit as a young curate, except when I was on holiday. I used to be a little shocked to see some priests from the diocese of Westminster, which included London, putting on a collar and a tie to go out in the evenings.

As well as saying daily Mass and the administration of the sacraments, parish visiting was the big thing. Young curates were expected to be out every day, visiting the Catholics of the parish. I would meet the gasman and the rent collector, all, like me, doing their rounds, visiting the families in these little houses. I was given a list of the Catholics living in the area around the church but I found that it was hopelessly out of date. I decided I would create a new one. So I went round, knocking on every door, in street after street, doing a census of the Catholic families. Although we had 700 or 800 people at Mass every Sunday, I soon found that most of the Catholics in the parish were no longer coming to church – they were lapsed. I was surprised to discover that they knew very little about the teaching of the Church or about the sacraments. They had been baptized. They might have gone to a Catholic school. But in many cases that was about it.

It began to dawn on me that I had a mountain to climb. I was beginning to realize that there were a lot of Catholics in the parish who would go to church once a month, or once a year. In Italy, there were many men who would not darken the doors of a church except for a *festa*; Pius XII advised priests who were about to preach retreats during Lent not to have a go at them for missing Mass on a Sunday, because in their own minds these men would not have thought of it as being a mortal sin. After about three years I started to bring small groups of people together. I would give them little talks about the Gospel, and I would talk about Jesus, and then we used to talk together about the faith. Gradually, I was coming to realize that 'church' meant little to them and that somehow it was necessary, if faith was to become alive, for them to encounter the Word of God, not only in scripture but also in the experience of other believers. This was the germ of the idea that I would develop later.

One of my roles was to be the chaplain to the girls' grammar school. Once a week I had to speak about the faith for three-quarters of an hour to bright and inquisitive 12- to 18-year-old girls. Another job was to lead the 'Padre Hour' – giving instruction to men doing their National Service at a nearby barracks. I felt sorry for these young soldiers, being marched in once a week, tired and weary, to listen to me spouting on. The lectures in philosophy and theology I had sat through at the Greg proved pretty useless in helping me find a way of engaging these young people. I had to look elsewhere for inspiration. My parish priest might have been a little laid-back, but he was also a bit of a scholar, and had a decent library. So in my first five years as a priest I spent a lot of time reading, helping me to relate my studies in Rome to the realities of parish life.

On Saturday afternoons I played rugby for Portsmouth. I made some very good friends among the rugby fraternity, in particular John Vail, who with his wife Anne and family became life-long friends. Although at 6 feet 3 inches in height you might think my natural habitat was in the pack, I used to prefer messing around in the backs. I don't think the bishop was entirely happy about it. I had to return to the parish for evening confessions, so I was usually only able to stay for a quick beer after a match. Towards the end of one season we entered the Havant Sevens. We were complete no-hopers really, but somehow we got through the pool stages. Then to my astonishment – mixed with alarm – we won our quarter-final. This was getting tricky; the clock was ticking. Then we won the semi-final. And then the final! Unprecedented. And very awkward. Eventually, I sprinted back to church. There was a queue as long as your arm of irate parishioners waiting for confession.

I wasn't a natural at rugby, like my brother Jim, but I was a tryer. Perhaps you could say the same for my efforts at public speaking. I knew about the work of the Catholic Evidence Guild, which trained speakers to explain the faith in public places, prominently of course at Speakers' Corner in Hyde Park. I thought I'd give it a go on the seafront at Southsea. I set up my soap box and a big crowd gathered, but hecklers interrupted my carefully polished talks, and I wasn't sharp or witty enough to respond in kind. After a few minutes, people used to drift away. It was humiliating, but good experience. And I consoled myself by remembering the passage in John's gospel that describes how on one occasion when Jesus was speaking to a large crowd, it was too much for a number of them: 'and after this, many of his disciples left him and stopped going with him' (John 6.65). I was not alone in not being listened to. I had more success with a series of talks I gave for non-Catholics at a nearby hall. It was well advertised and a large number came to the meetings; twenty or so were later received into full communion with the Church.

The union of Christians? Ecumenism was simply not a priority or in the forefront of our minds in those days, though I was glad to become friendly with a number of Anglican clergy in that area. I remember the first occasion I went to a meeting of all the leaders of the churches and Christian communities in the North End area. A venerable Congregationalist minister was asked to open our meeting with prayer. He looked around the room, and he prayed for everyone there, his brothers the Anglican ministers, and the Baptist and the Methodist ministers, and then his eye caught mine. 'And let us pray even for our Roman Catholic brother here present.' Those were early days.

The parish priest had a car. I had a bicycle. It served me well. It was ideal for getting to know people in the parish. If you walk, well, you've always got to stop and talk to parishioners when you see them; and if you have a car, you can't, whether you want to or not. If you're on a bicycle you can do either one or the other. After four years, I managed to scrape together £60 to buy a car. It was a 1936 Austin Ruby. It had curtains and flashing direction indicators that flicked out from the sides. It was my first car and I was very fond of it, but soon the brakes disintegrated and I had to get rid of it.

I'd go home to my mother and father in Reading as often as I could, usually once a week for lunch. It was quite a difficult hike in those days, I had to change trains twice. Pat would try to be there too, though Brian's parish was on the Isle of Wight, a five-hour journey away, so he couldn't always make it. John was away, serving in the Army. Jim was very busy with his practice. The eight of us never met all together as a family again after my ordination in 1956. By the time I came back from Rome my father's heart trouble had got worse. He had retired from work in the practice and my mother was pretty much devoted to looking after him.

1960 was a sad year for the family. My father died in February. I still remember my mother standing around the bed with her five sons. We were saying the rosary at the moment of his death. In my mind, my father was a saintly figure, steadfast in faith and unsparing in charity; his life was spent in serving his family, his patients and the community. Then, entirely unexpectedly, my brother John was diagnosed with cancer. He died in November. He loved being a soldier; he was the life and soul of every party. We were heartbroken. The Lord has strange ways. I still mourn John's loss.

I got to know the people in the parish in the North End of Portsmouth very well. But I was frustrated there. I felt pretty powerless. Looking back on those early years in the priesthood, I am conscious of how immature I was in many ways. I had unrealistic hopes and expectations. I was increasingly conscious of what Mother Teresa once said: 'God has not called me to be successful – he has called me to be faithful.' When my first holiday came along at last, I had this great feeling of being free. After Rome, life in Portsmouth felt narrow and limited, and I started to feel miserable, perhaps even a little depressed. After the fellowship of the seminary, parish life could be lonely. I began to understand some of the pressures felt by priests, and it was a lesson I never forgot.

In 1962 I got word that I was going to be asked to join the Catholic Missionary Society, a group of priests from different dioceses who gave retreats and preached missions in parishes all over the country. I thought this way of life would suit me very well and I was looking forward to joining the work. However, it was not to be. Instead, Archbishop King suddenly decided that I was needed elsewhere, and to my disappointment I was moved to the parish of the Sacred Heart in Fareham, a large sprawling parish that covered much of the area between Portsmouth and Southampton. I hadn't wanted to go, but it is a strange fact that what appears at first to be a setback sometimes turns out to be a blessing in disguise. It was to be in Fareham that I began to find my feet.

In 1960 Thomas Holland had been appointed coadjutor to Archbishop King, who was then 79. The idea was that he would soon take over the reins, but King rather woke up again at Tommy's appearance and didn't let him do anything really. He was told to go round the diocese visiting all the convents. It was a frustrating time for him. It was Tommy who made me vocations director for the diocese. He kept ringing different priests trying to cajole them into doing it and they kept saying, 'No, no, no'. Finally he turned to me and said: 'Cormac, I think you'll have to do it.' The job meant going round all the Catholic schools in Hampshire and Berkshire talking to the boys about the priesthood. I enjoyed it more than I expected.

In the early 1960s there was still – just – a sense among Catholics that the life of a priest was something special. When I gave a talk to 11- or 12-year-olds and asked, 'Who wants to be a priest?', pretty well all of them would put up their hands. That wouldn't happen now. And even when I spoke to boys in the sixth form, who would all look suitably bored, after I'd finished talking there would always be two or three who would quietly come to see me afterwards. I would hold retreats for small groups of boys who showed an interest, or we would go away for a weekend somewhere. The boys could realize that they were not alone, that there were others who were thinking the same way. Declan Lang, who was later to become the bishop of Clifton, was one of them.

I found that the best foundation for the priesthood was prayer and doing something for others. When people would ask me how to pray, I would suggest, don't be afraid to just stop and listen for a minute or two. Just sit in silence for a few moments. You don't have to talk to God all the time. Be still, and listen. Let God speak to you in your heart. It's in silence that we meet God. I would tell them to just keep at it. Basil Hume used to call it 'the prayer of incompetence'. Like all of us, he often didn't get much satisfaction or consolation out of prayer and he would feel his prayer just wasn't any good. But he just kept praying. And that's the best advice, really. Just keep praying.

Among my other duties I was chaplain to a nearby psychiatric hospital and this led to a new experience of meeting patients and trying to understand something more about mental illness. In those days the practice of lobotomy was widely performed on patients. I had doubts about its efficacy then and I still do today, though I cannot claim any expertise in the matter. But, again, this was an area of life which I had not experienced before and I found my meetings with the patients, especially those who recently had come for treatment, was very helpful and instructive for my experience of life.

There are events in the life of a priest that are extraordinarily joyful and there are moments which are desperately sad. I will never forget one evening when I was attending a meeting of one of the small groups of parishioners which was part of the parish renewal. Among those present were a couple who had just come down from the north of England and had settled in Fareham with their two young children. After the meeting, they left to go home and at 10.30 the husband, who was not a Catholic, went out to begin his night shift. At half past eleven, when I was asleep, I got a call from the hospital. He had been in a serious accident. I got dressed and went to the hospital, where I met his wife, distraught, helpless, waiting to see if her husband would live or die. I stayed with her at the hospital all night long. At 4 o'clock, we were told that her husband had died. She was completely alone, and I had to help and comfort her in any way that I could. I couldn't find the right words to say. There aren't any, really, for these sorts of situations. All I could do was be there. It was one of those tragedies that happen in life. One of the privileges and consolations of a priest is to be part of great sorrow and just to be present, a sign of support and, in some mysterious way, of the Providence and the love of God. After a little while, she and her children went back to the north and she was able to begin a new life.

There were also very happy times which I spent with the parish youth club. The club used to meet every week and it was, of course, the time when the Beatles were all in vogue. Every week, at our gathering, Beatles songs would be hammered out and the young people would jive and sing and I got to know and like them very much indeed. Towards the end of my time in the parish I wrote a gospel song for the musicians of the youth club, which they played at a competition for all the Christian youth clubs in Hampshire. On the day of the competition, which was held at Beaulieu in the New Forest, a large crowd assembled and fourteen or fifteen youth clubs each performed their gospel song. There were three judges and the winning song was to be decided not only by the judges but also by the enthusiasm of the crowd. I had arranged for a busload or two of supporters to travel to the event and, of course, our song duly earned great applause and eventually was declared the winner. The song, 'Come ye Blessed of my Father', was put into a gospel songbook and actually earned me a tidy sum in royalties.

I was becoming more deeply involved in the life of the people of the parish. I was conducting baptisms and weddings and funerals. I was going around all the schools talking about priesthood and going on retreats with young people. I was working with people with mental illness. I was spending time with the old and the sick. I would meet a lovely married couple with their three children and then learn that they were having difficulties in their marriage. I was beside people at the most joyful and most painful and devastating moments of their lives. We still had our mission – the long-term vision of the conversion of England, and the task in the meantime of 'keeping the faith'. Mass, confessions, benedictions were all good, but I was starting to feel that we had to do more than just keeping the show going, minding the shop. Something more like renewal was needed. And my experiences were starting to tell me that renewal would only come from the bottom up.

I had come from a relatively comfortable middle-class home, had had a privileged education in Rome, and there was I going round from house to house, often to poor families, saying, 'You ought to come back to Mass'. I came to realize that I might have got things the wrong way round. Before people could be brought back to a sacramental life, they had to be brought back to the Gospel, to some experience of the community of the Church, and this could only happen if they were to meet people like themselves who were trying to live as Christians. Theological inspiration came from a book by Yves Congar, a French Dominican priest, called *Lay People in the Church,* first published in English in 1965. Congar emphasized how at the heart of the Church, like cells, were little groups of people bonded together and with the grace of the Holy Spirit, willing them to become alert to the promptings of God in their daily life. The Church would be renewed by small communities of lay people committed to living out their faith in everyday life.

I thought, 'Let's try it'. My fellow curate and I got up ten small groups, meeting once a month in people's homes. There were strict rules. No elaborate meals. No showing off. Just tea and biscuits. People read a passage from the Bible together, and prayed together. They talked about their working lives, shared their experiences as parents, as husbands and wives, as divorced people or single people. These groups were unusual at that time. It was not the norm for parishioners to meet in each others' homes and talk about their faith and the effect it had on their lives. The parish priest wasn't particularly keen, but he agreed to go along with it.

Some of the groups worked better than others. There were always some people who wanted to do all the talking, or people who said the same thing over and over at every meeting, and people who said they would come but always failed to turn up. I think the groups worked better in Fareham, a more prosperous area, than they would have done in my first parish, where many people would have felt uncomfortable at the thought of people coming to their homes for meetings. But the idea spread. It was a big parish, we'd have perhaps a thousand at Mass, and we got to the point were we had 250 belonging to one or other of the groups. People were meeting to talk to each other about their faith, trying to link it to their own lives. After four years the groups had made a transformation. It had become a 'living' parish.

These groups were an eye-opener for me. There was a dawning realization that we are in some mysterious way in communion as brothers and sisters. Deep within us we long to connect with people. We have all experienced the pain of communion, the pain of tension and conflict, of loss, of heartbreak. Parents and children long for peace in the home. We all need to be loved, to be taken into account. It hurts when we feel we are forgotten, left out, excluded. Jesus knew what it was to long for community when he prayed, 'May they all be one, Father, just as you are in me and I am in you, so that they may also be in us, so that the world may believe it was you who sent me' (John 17.21). It was the beginning of a more profound understanding of the Church, living and lived, in the hearts and souls of faithful people. It also changed my understanding of the priesthood. By participating in these discussions, I discovered why I as a priest needed lay people to teach me new insights into a living faith, just as they needed me as a priest to be a sign and guide to the realities of the Church in the midst of their world. These experiences remained with me, and when, in later years, I became a bishop, I tried to translate them in the wider sphere of a diocese.

After I discovered the small groups, the first thing I would say to lapsed Catholics was not 'Come back to Mass' but 'Come and meet a small group of fellow Catholics'. I remember many years later talking to Basil Hume about this. He didn't really agree with me when I launched an initiative to introduce small groups into the Arundel and Brighton diocese when I was bishop there. He thought the sacraments should come first; my experience has been that you've got to hear the Gospel first and have some experience of what the Christian life looks and tastes like, by seeing it in front of your nose – then you celebrate what you hear and experience of the Gospel in the liturgy and in the sacraments. The astonishing and heartening success of the Alpha course seems to bear this out. Its leader, Nicky Gumbel, has latched on to Congar's basic idea and used it not only to pack the comfortable middle classes of Kensington and Chelsea into Holy Trinity Brompton but to bring huge numbers of people from every background to a discovery or rediscovery of Christianity.

The four years I spent in Fareham from 1963 overlapped, of course, with the years of the second Vatican Council, which had opened in 1962 and ended in 1965. Good and brave Pope John XXIII had called a Council, bringing together the bishops of the Church from every corner of the world. The goal was *aggiornamento*, the 'bringing up to date' of the Church. I suspect Pope John just had an instinct that this was a moment for the Church to reflect on its mission and its relationship to the world so that its message could become more effective. Even during the years when I was a student in Rome, theologians were beginning to be restless under the restrictions placed on their reflections on the place of the Church in the modern world. So the Council appeared, especially to young people, and particularly to a young priest like me, as a breath of fresh air. It was to be a catalyst for change and renewal for a Church in danger of becoming isolated in its own certitudes and less able to communicate the Good News of the Gospel not only to our own faithful but also to the wider world, which also had 'ears to hear, and minds to discover' the newness of the message and promises of the Lord.

I eagerly followed the course of the Council, absorbing as best I could the great documents on the Liturgy, the Church, on Revelation, on Ecumenism, on human rights and religious freedom and on the Church in the modern world. The first and most dramatic impact the Council made on the ordinary life of the parish was in the celebration of the Sunday Mass in English rather than in Latin. It is said that 'the eucharist makes the Church and the Church makes the eucharist'. For the majority of Catholics, Mass on Sunday was where they encountered the scriptures and the life of the Church. As the opening words of the Council's document on the liturgy point out:

> It is the liturgy through which, especially in the divine sacrifice of the Eucharist, the work of our redemption is accomplished, and it is through the liturgy, especially, that the faithful are able to express in their lives and manifest to others the mystery of Christ and the real nature of the true Church. The liturgy daily builds up those who are in the Church, making of them a holy temple of the Lord, and a dwelling-place for God in the Spirit.

Gradually the celebration of the Mass in English with the priest facing the people, rather than with his back to them, became the norm. The main purpose of the changes was to ensure active participation of all the people in the celebration of the sacrament. Slowly, this began to be fulfilled. Of all the changes brought about by the second Vatican Council, those to the liturgy had the most immediate effect on the Catholic people as a whole. There were, of course, a minority who hungered after the old Tridentine rite of the Mass and in 1971 Cardinal Heenan, with the approval of Pope Paul, ensured that some provision could be made on special occasions for this group.

By the time the Mass in the vernacular was being introduced, my time in Fareham was coming to an end. After my experiences as a curate in two parishes, I was beginning to mature and to realize more deeply what priesthood actually means. Priesthood is not just presiding at Mass and administering the sacraments and preaching on Sundays, it is somehow to be a living sign of Christ in the whole Body of the Church. Although the priest has many things to do, perhaps his most important function is, through prayer and presence, with the people always in his heart, to root the Church in a particular place, at a particular time and with particular people.

In 1965 our bishop, John Henry King, who was well into his 80s, died. The man who had been appointed his coadjutor, Tommy Holland, had been moved on to Salford the previous year. A frisson passed through the clergy of the Portsmouth diocese when they learnt who had been appointed to be our new bishop. We'd all heard of Derek Worlock. He had been secretary to three cardinals and had been present at all the sessions of the Council. He was reputed to be a force of nature. Life was going to be very different for all of us. Especially for me. Within six months, Derek asked me to leave parish life to live and work with him as his secretary.

4

A breath of fresh air

In the summer of 1956, a few months before I was ordained, I decided to visit Venice. I will never forget arriving in the evening in a vaporetto and crossing the Grand Canal. The lights were shining, the water beamed, and St Mark's Basilica was silhouetted in the foreground – it was magical. It was the eve of the feast of St Laurence Giustiniani, the first Patriarch of Venice and, along with St Mark, its principal patron. The next morning I went to St Mark's Square and watched as the current Patriarch arrived in a gondola to celebrate the festal Mass. This was my first sight of Angelo Roncalli – being rowed towards St Mark's Square by four gondoliers. When I entered the basilica I found that, while the Patriarch was presiding in choir dress, the actual celebrant was the Archbishop of Milan, Giovanni Baptista Montini. Roncalli had obviously invited Montini to Venice for the ceremonies. I remember after the Mass was over, he and Montini came out onto the balcony of the basilica. Everybody in the square cheered and clapped their beloved Patriarch, but Roncalli stepped back, gently nudged Montini forward and made a gesture to the people. 'Clap *him*,' he seemed to be saying, 'this man is going to be the next pope.'

Little did Roncalli realize that within two years it would be him who would be elected to the papacy and to take the name John XXIII, to be followed by the younger Montini, who would succeed him in 1963 as Pope Paul VI. He very soon became 'Good Pope John'. Pope John was a breath of fresh air. He was once asked by a visiting diplomat how many people worked at the Vatican. 'About half', he replied. He was simple, humorous, shrewd – and a man of great faith. He trusted in the Lord, whom he loved. And he himself was to become greatly loved. Few popes had visited the Regina Coeli Prison; none had introduced himself to the prisoners as 'Giuseppe, your brother'.

And then of course, within a few months of his election, he did something dramatic and unexpected. He called a second Vatican Council. It came as a great shock to many in the Vatican. Cardinal Montini remarked to a friend: 'This holy old boy does not realize what a hornet's nest he has stirred up.' The Council was to be the most important event in the history of the Church in the twentieth century. It stimulated and shaped the mission of the Church in the years that followed. It was an extraordinary grace and gift of God to the Church, and I suspect that the teaching of the Council has, even now, not yet been fully grasped and that its long-term effects have yet to emerge.

I was 30 years old and six years ordained a priest, and was coming to the end of my time in my first parish in North End, Portsmouth, when the Vatican Council opened in October 1962. Looking back now, fifty years later, it is difficult to recreate the extraordinary effect of the Council on the Church in England. For me, the Council was a great enrichment in my Christian life and a new beginning for the Church and, as I have said in the previous chapter, I followed its progress avidly. I eagerly read the reports of the proceedings in Rome but I particularly enjoyed the 'goings on' behind the scenes related with gossipy intimacy by Xavier Rynne, the pseudonym of the late Francis X. Murphy, an American priest teaching in Rome who was close to many of the bishops and expert advisers attending the Council sessions. Rynne's 'Letters from Vatican City', originally published in *The New Yorker*, had colourful character sketches of the great reforming heroes of the Council and described their efforts to outmanoeuvre the minority of cardinals who were stubbornly resistant to change. It was an epic struggle between the different factions at the Council, and he was clear where his sympathies lay.

All in all, I relished what was happening and although few of us really absorbed or fully understood the documents that emerged year after year, nevertheless the Council brought fresh hope and inspiration to me and to so many others here in England and Wales. The aims of the Council were made clear in the opening paragraph of the very first document that was issued, *Sacrosanctum Concilium*, the Constitution on the Sacred Liturgy, which was approved by the assembled bishops by a vote of 2,147 to 4 and promulgated by Pope Paul VI on 4 December 1963:

> The Sacred Council has set out to impart an ever-increasing vigour to the Christian life of the faithful; to adapt more closely to the needs of our age those institutions which are subject to change; to foster whatever can promote union among all who believe in Christ and to strengthen whatever can help to call all people into the embrace of the Church.

I was inspired and bowled over by these words. The bishops of the Council were declaring a new pastoral approach to Christian life, a renewal of the institution of the Church so that it would speak to the hopes and dreams of modern men and women. They were demanding ecumenism and a quest for the unity of Christians and they were calling for a new evangelization. It was heady stuff.

I'll spare you my personal commentary on the individual documents of Vatican II – there have been very many books on each of them. There were, as I've said, some key documents that reflected the main themes of the Council. Apart from the Constitution on the Liturgy, the Constitution on the Church, *Lumen Gentium*, was devoted to a new way of looking at the Church itself. By beginning the document with the concept of the People of God, the bishops made a clear and challenging statement about the nature of the Church itself. We used to think of 'the Church' as the pope, the hierarchy, priests and nuns and only then the laity. *Lumen Gentium* made it clear that the Church was made up of all God's people and that all are equally called to holiness. From this came the concept of the co-responsibility of all the faithful for the mission of the Church. We are all in this together. The role of the laity, of all the baptized, is crucial in the life of the Church. The Pastoral Constitution on the Church in the Modern World delineated a new relationship between the Church and the world. Its Latin title, *Gaudium et Spes*, was taken from its opening words, 'joy and hope', and set the mood. The language and tone were strikingly, refreshingly different from the encyclical letters of Popes Pius XI and Pius XII that I'd been used to studying – without great enthusiasm – as a student in Rome in the 1950s. It made it clear that the Church does not pretend to have all the answers to the questions that confront society. It is, rather, a companion on the journey for all humankind, whose destiny it is to create the history of this world. It does not set out the precise relationship between the secular world and the Kingdom of God, but that the two are closely related – and are not at war with each other – is taken as read. When I became a bishop, twelve years after it was written, I took as my motto 'Gaudium et Spes', a reference to a document which still remains in many ways unfinished business.

These were some of the thoughts I took with me as I began my new work as secretary and assistant to Derek Worlock. He was a remarkable man, an extraordinarily good organizer with a meticulous and retentive memory. He was totally dedicated to his work and, having been personal secretary to three Archbishops of Westminster, was well acquainted with the ways and means of bringing matters to a satisfactory conclusion. Derek had been present at the Council, first as secretary to the English and Welsh bishops and finally, to his great satisfaction, as a *peritus*, or theological expert. He saw himself, not unreasonably, as the person best qualified to bring the insights and teaching of the Council to the people of England and Wales and, in particular, the people of his diocese. He was clearly a man who had ambitions, for the diocese, for the church and indeed, in an understandable and honourable way, for himself.

Derek had not been Cardinal Heenan's first choice as Archbishop King's successor. Heenan had been appointed Archbishop of Westminster in September 1963, and although Derek took over as his private secretary, Heenan soon moved him on to Whitechapel, in London's East End, where he became a parish priest. 'He scarcely used me and never told me what he was up to', Derek wrote later. Perhaps Heenan recognized that there was only room for one leader in Archbishop's House. When towards the end of the Council John Petit, the Bishop of Menevia, who was 70 and had a huge diocese that stretched over north Wales, said he needed a coadjutor bishop with the right to succeed him, I think Heenan thought to himself, 'Here's a chance to get Derek even further away, into the mountains of Wales'. But what apparently happened was that when Heenan told other senior figures in the hierarchy at the English College during the final session of the Council that it had been decided in Rome that Langton Fox, who was the rector of the seminary in Wonersh, would be going to Portsmouth and that Derek would be going to Wales, they said, 'You can't send Derek off to Menevia, it's just not fair, not right'. So Heenan, who was a member of the Congregation for Bishops, arranged for them to be swapped round. When the announcement came, it was Langton Fox who would be appointed to Wales, and Derek who would be coming to Portsmouth. He was consecrated as the fifth bishop of Portsmouth in the cathedral on 21 December 1965.

When Derek invited me to be his secretary the following summer, I had been ordained nine years and was due to become a parish priest. A bit of me was quite pleased to be asked. Every bishop had a priest-secretary, and they would pick someone they thought would be capable and who they could get on with. The role involved living with the bishop, driving him around to meetings and events in the diocese, and being a sort of liaison between him and the priests. Derek knew the Murphy-O'Connors. He would meet my father on the national pilgrimage to Lourdes every year – George was the official doctor, and Derek would be there as Cardinal Griffin's secretary. When my father died in 1960 there was a lovely letter to my mother from Griffin's successor, Cardinal Godfrey, but probably written by Derek. He knew I'd been a student in Rome, and he wanted someone who might be able to understand Italian a bit and be at ease in the Vatican. Or perhaps he thought there wasn't much to choose from. I always remember, the first time we went together to Rome, they were announcing the names of the people who were to be appointed as consultors to the new Council for the Laity. I can still see us standing there and when someone called out 'Worlock!' his face lit up – he was thrilled to bits. It was his first official appointment in Rome since being appointed a bishop.

I'd already seen Derek in action. I was once asked to represent the diocese at a meeting that Cardinal Godfrey had called in Westminster to encourage the creation of Catholic youth clubs. It was a new initiative, and almost certainly one of Derek's bright ideas. Derek came in with Godfrey and the cardinal welcomed us all, but then he disappeared. I thought, when is the cardinal coming back? But he never did. Derek ran the meeting very briskly and efficiently. I was impressed. I remember at the end he asked: 'Any questions?' There was silence before one of the priests said: 'What about my expenses?' Derek was stony-faced. He was not in the first rank as a humorist.

The four years I spent with Derek were very formative for me. There was the everyday work of visitation of parishes, arranging interviews, taking notes at meetings and keeping the diary. I helped to draft and comment on his many speeches and addresses. With Derek you were always able to put your oar in. Often we would be away together, staying overnight somewhere in the diocese, or in London or Rome, and sometimes we would only touch base in the cathedral house for a few days before being off on our travels again. Nothing was too much trouble for Derek and the schedule was exhausting, but, all in all – and a little to my surprise – I found that we worked well together.

We had been fortunate to obtain the services of three Sisters of Mercy to run the household. The sister deputed to cook was very much a novice in the art. One evening she cooked sausage rolls and baked beans. Ever the encourager, I thanked her profusely and said how much I had enjoyed it. Soon afterwards, Derek invited the Mayor, an Admiral of the Fleet, and a third guest to dinner. We only returned from an engagement an hour or two before the meal, so I had not been able to check the menu, but I had selected some good wine for the occasion, and we laid the table with our best cutlery and china. We sat down for dinner and ate a small first course, and then our cook proudly served the main dish – sausage rolls and baked beans! Derek's face was a study but the Admiral rose to the occasion. 'Wonderful! What a splendid change. Though I have to say', he said, looking over at me, 'I'm not convinced this wine is an entirely suitable complement to these magnificent baked beans.'

Sleep didn't come easily to Derek. He was always up early in the morning, and he worked non-stop. He wanted to be involved in everything. He knew everything and everyone. He was at every meeting, chairing or taking the minutes, the great fixer and deal-maker and manipulator. He would get angry sometimes, but he never lost his rag in public. And he was very austere. He never ate very much. And if we had wine with a meal, he'd stick at half a glass of white. He smoked, although I think in the end he gave it up. In those days I still smoked myself, though never very much.

Derek had a great need for companionship. He liked to have somebody with him the whole time. He could be difficult; he could be vain, and perhaps a little bit of a bully sometimes. No doubt he was something of what we'd call nowadays 'a control freak'. He always knew exactly where he was going. If he went to a meeting, he was always well prepared. Whatever came up, he seemed to have a note prepared that he could refer to. But a lovely thing about Derek was that it didn't matter to him whether it was Cardinal so-and-so or Mrs Bloggs who asked him for help. He'd give as much attention to one as to the other. He was meticulous about that. He wasn't secretive; he shared pretty well everything. He used to talk everything over with me, and it was a sort of initiation and a formation in how to run a diocese.

Derek always tried to be flexible. He would always try to manoeuvre things, to find a solution whenever he could. But though he would always try to be compassionate and imaginative in how he interpreted them, the rules were the rules. It was an instinct I shared. He was usually very good with priests who were in any sort of personal trouble. But he was not always a very good judge of character. I think he took priests into the diocese he shouldn't have, people who had caused trouble in other dioceses or with their religious superiors, and they usually caused trouble when they came in. I think he did it out of compassion. Behind the reserve and the shyness he wanted to be a compassionate bishop. I can't blame him for that; I've made similar mistakes myself.

One of the things I learnt from Derek was how to manage a meeting. He might seem to let them go on too long sometimes, but I saw how he would take care to bring people in, to make sure every voice was heard. The pastoral care of priests was a priority for him. And I learnt the importance of planning, of knowing what you want to achieve and how you might get there. You might have to adapt the plan in light of changing circumstances or after consulting people, but I've found it's best not to expect other people to come up with what you are supposed to do. You are there to give some kind of freshness to the things every bishop has to do. Soon after arriving, Derek chose twelve or fifteen of the brightest priests in the diocese and took them away for a meeting to plan for the future. Derek might have been a good planner, but he lacked self-awareness. After the meeting, he sent a letter to all the priests of the diocese saying something like, 'Now, let us begin ...'. They were not entirely pleased. 'Does he think we've been sitting around doing nothing for the past fifty years?'

Derek was a great enthusiast for the apostolate of the lay people. One of his driving passions was his belief that every baptized person had a precious role to play in the Church and in society. But one of the paradoxes of Derek was that while he was completely sincere in his conviction that lay people and clergy were equal partners in the mission of the Church, each with their own distinct contribution to make, temperamentally he liked to keep a close personal grip on things. Derek could never be involved in anything without wanting to be at the heart of it, without wanting to direct it. As Basil Hume once said, Derek was the only man he'd ever known who really, genuinely, always reads all the small print.

Derek promoted ecumenism in any way he could. On one occasion he and the Anglican Bishop of Portsmouth arranged a joint meeting of thirty clergy, fifteen a side. The weekend was a very convivial and fruitful one, but I was struck by the differences between the Anglican and Catholic clergy. The Anglicans, on the whole, seemed better informed and more clued up about the history and culture of their area; they were more likely to know the local councillors and the National Trust properties most worth a visit and be familiar with local societies. The Catholic priests, on the other hand, it seemed to me, were typically less engaged with the wider community but tended to be better read in theology and church history. To some extent I suppose these differences just reflected the fact that the Anglicans had all been to English universities whereas the Catholic formation had been solely in the seminary. These differences between Church of England and Catholic clergy would almost certainly not be replicated now – most Catholic priests these days were at university before they went on to prepare for the priesthood.

Ecumenical progress remained slow in some respects. In those days, Catholics were always expected to marry in a Catholic church with a Catholic priest officiating. So when the Anglican Bishop of Portsmouth's daughter was to be married to a Catholic naval officer it presented Derek with a difficult case. Naturally, the bishop wanted to preside at his daughter's wedding; he was not content just to be present and speak at a marriage in the groom's Catholic church. That wouldn't be a problem now, but in those days it was an awkward situation. The rule then was quite clear, and Derek played a straight bat. He explained to his Anglican counterpart that his daughter's wedding would have to take place in a Catholic church. The bride's father would be very welcome at the service, and would be invited to play a part, perhaps to pray or whatever, but the wedding would be presided over by a Catholic priest. When the Archbishop of Canterbury, Michael Ramsey, heard that Derek was insisting the marriage had to take place in a Catholic church, he was furious, and complained to the apostolic delegate about the intransigent and unecumenical attitude of the Roman Catholic Church and, in particular, of Bishop Derek Worlock. I was with Derek when a call came from the nuncio saying that Ramsey had complained about him to Rome. When Derek put the phone down, he immediately said: 'Right, Cormac. We're going to drive up to Lambeth.' I think he just picked up the phone to Ramsey's office and told them he was coming.

It was the first time I'd driven through the gatehouse and pulled in to park in front of the entrance to Lambeth Palace. We went in, and there at the top of the stairs was Ramsey, glowering down at the pair of us. I thought my man was in for a tough time. He and Derek went off for a private conversation. After about twenty minutes they came out. Derek wrote later that he had come up with a solution, later to be known as 'the Portsmouth solution': the marriage rite and the exchange of promises took place in the Catholic church in the morning, then there was a second celebration in the bride's church in the afternoon, with the bride's father presiding. Not perfect, perhaps, but a typical Derek fix. Since then, we've moved on. These days, dispensations from the Catholic form of marriage can be given and a Catholic and an

Anglican may be married in an Anglican church with the Anglican priest officiating.

People are always trying to sum up Derek Worlock. Was his refusal to admit failure in any enterprise his greatest strength or his greatest weakness? Derek certainly seemed to be driven by the need to be recognized, to be vindicated. He was always trying to prove himself. His father, Harford Worlock, had been a journalist before becoming a political agent for the Conservative Party in Winchester, and his mother was a suffragette. They were both converts; most of Derek's extended family were Anglicans, and several of his ancestors had been Anglican clergy. He was sent away to St Edmund's College in Ware – as a schoolboy and then a seminarian – from the age of 10. His older brother was killed early in the war. Like Basil Hume, who had decided in 1941 to enter a monastery as a novice rather than to serve in the armed forces, Derek elected to continue his studies for the priesthood rather than to join up; he was ordained in 1944, and became private secretary to Cardinal Griffin the following year. Derek's decision led to a slight estrangement from his father, though they were later to be reconciled. Basil Hume later told the story of how one of his contemporaries at Ampleforth who had left to join the Army had written to him at the end of the war to tell him, 'You can come out now – it's quite safe'. Young men like Derek and Basil had to make terrible choices which priests of my generation were lucky to have been spared. These things are always something of a mystery, but Derek's constant need to prove himself may have had its roots in a desire to make up for a father's disappointment.

Derek knew he wasn't going to stay in Portsmouth; as has often been said, Derek wanted to go to Westminster. That was quite clear from the beginning. That doesn't mean he didn't give everything to Portsmouth.

For the first year or so in Portsmouth, he did things other bishops didn't do: when Derek made a speech, for example, he would send a copy to the Catholic papers, so everyone would know what was happening in Portsmouth. Some of the priests in the diocese were reading the papers and saying, 'Gosh, I didn't know we were as good as that'.

When Heenan died in 1975, Worlock was first on the list in Rome to replace him, and he was confidently expecting it. He didn't realize that many of the priests in Westminster weren't keen on his return and had made their feelings known to the apostolic delegate, Bruno Heim. So when the news came that Basil Hume was to be the next Archbishop of Westminster it was a shock, although Rome tried to soften the blow by appointing Derek to the vacant see of Liverpool.

Derek felt the disappointment deeply, but set himself to make a success of Liverpool, which he did, triumphantly. And he was determined, too, that even though Basil would be the leader, it would be a partnership. There was always a bit of tension around Derek. He and Basil were very unlike each other, but Basil increasingly came to recognize that he couldn't do without Derek's help. He and Basil were like chalk and cheese, but Basil wasn't good at organizing and Derek was. The double appointment of Basil to Westminster and Derek to Liverpool turned out to be a blessing. They needed each other; and the Church in England and Wales needed them both.

Basil had an extraordinary personal influence as a spiritual leader, on the bishops' conference, on the Church, and as a national leader. He had charisma. But in terms of the Church in England and Wales it was Derek who had his hand on the tiller. He was the mastermind behind the National Pastoral Congress which was held in Liverpool in 1980. Only Derek could have pulled off something like that. It was he who, more than anyone, was at the forefront of translating the vision of the second Vatican Council into a reality for Catholics here. He was at the heart of everything.

Rome trusted Derek. He delivered. In some ways, from Rome's point of view, Basil could not always be relied upon to 'deliver'. If they wanted something done, a problem taken care of, it was Derek who could always be trusted to find a solution. Rome knew that once Derek got his teeth into a problem he would never let it go until he had mastered it. Derek was well known to Archbishop Giovanni Benelli, who was very close to Pope Paul and the most powerful figure in Rome at that time, and Derek was certainly considered as a possible head of a congregation in Rome, perhaps Prefect of the Sacred Congregation for the Clergy. It might have crossed Basil's mind that life might be a little easier if Derek was out of his hair. But Derek didn't want to go to Rome. He never really felt at home there. He could only barely get by in Italian, he never learnt the language properly. Derek was an Englishman to the core.

I learnt a huge amount from Derek, but after four years as his secretary I felt it was time for a move. I was exhausted from the constant travelling, and perhaps we were both ready for a rest from each other. It's a strange part of the priestly life, perhaps, but unlike other professions we don't have what you might call a 'career plan'. I have never sought a particular job or position. We take what we're given. In the late summer of 1970, Derek appointed me to the Immaculate Conception parish, Portswood, Southampton. With God's help, I have always been able to say: 'Here I am, Lord – I come to do your will.' The move to Portswood delighted me, and I looked forward to a long stint as a parish priest. But as it turned out, I was hardly able to settle into the parish. The following year was to be even more hectic for me than the four that I had spent as Derek's secretary, and was to end in a surprise appointment the following summer that took me away from the diocese and back to Rome for six years. Sometimes the Lord has other plans for us.

5

Cold blasts and sudden showers

As well as being the Bishop of Portsmouth, Derek was the first secretary to the bishops' conference – which had been established in 1967 – so in the years when I was working with him I often found myself in Archbishop's House, and I came to see a lot of Cardinal John Carmel Heenan. When he caught sight of me, he used to give me a look as if to say, 'What on earth are you doing here again?' But I was to become quite close to Heenan, and he was to play an important part in my life.

Although by this time Heenan's famous energy and dynamism had started to fade, there was still a bit of an aura about him. He was a national figure in a way that his predecessors as the Archbishop of Westminster had not been, at least not since the time of Cardinals Hinsley and Manning. Born in Ilford, Essex, of Irish Catholic parents – Heenan's father had worked in the Patent Office as a clerk – Heenan was a brilliant communicator, and was at least as well known as the Archbishop of Canterbury at the time, Michael Ramsey. As the energetic young head of the Catholic Missionary Society and then successively Bishop of Leeds – where his restless uprooting and reshuffling of priests from one parish to another earned the diocese the soubriquet 'the cruel see' – and Archbishop of Liverpool, he had been a forceful (some would say ruthless) administrator and a confident and tireless defender of the Church in pamphlets, newspaper articles, public speeches and radio broadcasts. Heenan was never afraid to stir the pot. He spoke out strongly on social matters and caused a furore when commenting on the radio on the blatant discrimination against Catholics that took place in Northern Ireland. His firm and resolute character was not to everyone's liking. He could be brusque and a bit of a know-all, but often the priests with whom he fell out most spectacularly would later testify to his kindness and concern for their personal welfare.

I remember writing a letter to Heenan soon after I had begun my work with Derek. I explained that a man had been to see me and, among other things, he had warned that he would shoot the Archbishop of Canterbury if the plan went ahead for him to be invited to preach in Westminster Cathedral. My correspondent was not an enthusiastic ecumenist. Two or three days later, I received a laconic reply from the Cardinal. 'Dear Father Murphy-O'Connor,' he wrote, 'Thank you for your letter. Do not worry. Those kinds of murders only occur in Canterbury Cathedral. Yours devotedly, John Card. Heenan.'

Heenan was a fierce defender of the Catholic Church. If the Church in England was no longer fighting for its survival, it still felt under threat and its leaders often acted as if they had their backs against the wall. Heenan's instinct was to protect its reputation and good name at all costs, lest ammunition be given to its enemies. He was of a generation of Catholics for whom the worst sin was 'giving scandal'. If there was dirty linen, it was best washed in private. It was a frame of mind that was to lead to trouble for his successors.

In some ways Heenan was a tragic figure, torn between an old Catholicism in its death throes and a new Catholicism struggling to be born. I was a young priest, enthusiastic about the promise of reform and renewal that the Vatican Council promised, yet I shared Heenan's trust in the authority of the Church. Perhaps I've always been a little unquestioning of the Church's authority – but I think that's more because I'm naturally trusting of authority, something I think I get from my childhood, rather than any sort of Catholic conditioning. If I had been brought up to do what I was told, it was in an atmosphere of love and playfulness and forgiveness. Of course we have a duty to ask questions, to look at the evidence, especially before we make important decisions. But while faith should never be blind, we would be caught up in endless prevarication and doubt if we weren't able to make leaps of faith. Looking back, I sometimes wonder if I wasn't a little too trusting. Was this a trait that was to lead me into difficulties later?

Heenan saw me as a kind of sounding board. One morning he threw a typescript across at me and said: 'Read this and tell me what you think of it.' The next morning, the first thing he asked was: 'Well, what did you think of it?' I hadn't even opened it. It was a draft of *Not the Whole Truth*, the first and much the better of the two volumes of autobiography Heenan was to write. I realized he very much wanted me to read it, so I spent the whole day going through it. The next morning I was able to say: 'Your Eminence, I really enjoyed your book. I especially liked the family background and the account of your happy Catholic childhood in Ilford …' Then I thought I'd change tack. Heenan had visited Russia in 1936, disguised as a psychologist. It was a very daring thing to do. While he was in Moscow, Heenan had befriended a young student called Lola, a girl of exceptional courage, who had shown him around the city and revealed to him that she was a secret believer. It's quite clear from Heenan's text that Lola had fallen for this rather dashing young visitor, who had not been able to tell her that he was a Catholic priest.

'I enjoyed the chapter on Russia,' I said, 'I was just wondering ... what happened to Lola?' Heenan gave me an inscrutable look.

I don't think Heenan was ever really happy in Westminster. As he found, and as Basil Hume and I were to discover later, when you are in Westminster it's not an easy job. The first years after the end of the Council were particularly difficult and stressful, and his health began to fail. Heenan was suspicious of 'lay theologians', and he didn't much like the clerical sort either. It hurt him when priests and theologians criticized the teaching of the Church. For him, the great virtues were loyalty and obedience. He had set up a college to educate priests and laity, Corpus Christi, but was horrified by the radical theology that was taught there. There were rows and resignations and eventually the college was closed down. There was a growing feeling that things were running out of control. Heenan had come to believe, as he wrote in the closing pages of the second volume of autobiography, *A Crown of Thorns*, that, 'A bitter attack on the Catholic Church was mounted by her own children'.

What most distressed him was that priests, sometimes friends and often men he knew personally, were beginning to leave the priesthood. I happened to be in Archbishop's House in December 1966 when the news came that Charles Davis, perhaps the outstanding English Catholic theologian of the day, was to leave the priesthood and the Church. There was astonishment and consternation all around. Heenan was pulling on a cigarette and looking shaken. It was a terrific shock.

I had the sense that he was heartbroken, and close to despair. He couldn't understand how a man could leave the priesthood. In those last years, all the verve and assurance seemed to have gone. It wasn't so much the teaching of the Church that had changed, it was more the attitude of people to authority. That was the big shift. Before, when a bishop issued a statement, Catholics wouldn't question it. When a bishop decided to move a priest to a new parish, he might grumble but he wouldn't dream of refusing to budge. Catholic laity and priests did what they were told. This was the Church Heenan had been raised in and suddenly it seemed to be collapsing around him.

Then on 29 July 1968 there occurred the event that shook the Catholic world to its foundations: the publication of Pope Paul VI's encyclical letter on the regulation of birth, *Humanae Vitae*. I was on holiday with my brothers Pat and Brian at Palazzola. It was all over the news. People couldn't talk about anything else. All means of contraception, not only the contraceptive sheath but the Pill, were prohibited. From the terrace of the villa we could see the helicopter that took Pope Paul from the Vatican to his summer retreat at Castel Gandolfo, on the other side of the valley from us, almost as if he was escaping from the furore his letter had unleashed. It was the tourists and pilgrims in Rome who seemed most exercised by it. The Italians tended to shrug their shoulders, as if encyclicals came and went, and were not to be taken entirely seriously. In England, though, the encyclical was taken very seriously indeed. Derek was soon on the phone. 'I want you to come home immediately; we must prepare our pastoral letter.'

We got together in Birmingham with a small group of trusted friends of Derek's. There was general confusion and amazement. In the months before the encyclical was released Heenan had seemed to be preparing the ground for a change in the Church's position on the use of artificial contraception. But I was shocked by the strength of the reaction to the encyclical. This was something quite new. It was the 'silly season' for the media and the press had a field day with headlines about dissenting priests and dismay among Catholic laity. There was a letter to *The Times* signed by fifty-five priests challenging the teaching. An editorial in *The Tablet* came out against it.

The bishops were issuing pastoral letters supporting the papal teaching with varying degrees of enthusiasm. There was real tension between them. Some of them were untroubled by all the fuss. It was a simple matter of giving unconditional obedience to whatever the papal teaching was. Cyril Cowderoy, the Archbishop of Southwark, disappeared for a few days at the height of the crisis, with his diocese riven by ructions among the priests. When he came back, Derek happened to meet him. 'I'm very sorry, your Grace, for all the trouble you've been having', he said. The archbishop stroked his stomach. 'Oh, that's all right, Derek,' he said, 'my tummy is feeling much better now.' But other bishops, including Archbishop George Beck of Liverpool and Heenan's auxiliary bishop in Westminster, the former abbot of Downside, Christopher Butler, were having difficulties with some aspects of the encyclical. While not wanting to dissent publicly from the teaching of the pope, they were agonizing about how to find a formula which would allow priests and lay people who found themselves unable to follow the argument of the encyclical to still receive the sacraments.

Derek and I were reading all the pastoral letters as they came out, scanning them closely to see what their line would be. I helped him prepare his own pastoral letter. We sought a way to balance pastoral compassion with holding the Vatican position. We were able to do it by taking into account Catholic moral teaching regarding situations that are objectively sinful but also the subjective dispositions of faithful Christian men and women. It was Derek who came up with the phrase to describe acceptance of the teaching of *Humanae Vitae* as 'not the acid test of Christianity'. It helped us keep the affair in a wider context at an incredibly heated and difficult time. One priest in the diocese was suspended for speaking publicly against the encyclical by the vicar general while Derek was away, but when Derek returned he was quietly reinstated. Derek never suspended any priests in the diocese for dissent from the Church's teaching on this issue.

It was an awful time, and Heenan was stuck in the middle. In his famous television interview with David Frost, he defended the teaching of the encyclical. When Frost pressed him for what a priest should say to a Catholic couple who, after having properly informed their consciences, had decided to use the contraceptive pill, I remember holding my breath before Heenan answered: 'I would say, God bless you.' He went on to say that a couple who used contraception should follow their consciences in the matter. Heenan's reply established the tone for the approach the Church in England and Wales would take to the issue of contraception. It was, perhaps, a very English solution.

For my part, I have never dissented from the teaching of *Humanae Vitae*. I knew the terrible difficulties and heart-searching it created for many good Catholics, many of whom were torn, perhaps for the first time in their lives, between their consciences and the teaching of the Church. The issue for me was always, the Church has spoken: now how do I help my bishop communicate its teaching and to interpret it pastorally and with compassion and sensitivity as best we could.

My sense that *Humanae Vitae* could not be lightly dismissed was partly due to my sense of obedience to the magisterium of the Church, but also to my instinctive understanding of the inseparable connection of the unitive and procreative meaning (to use churchy language) of sexual intercourse. It seemed to me, even then, that it would be difficult to have a coherent teaching of the purpose of human sexuality if these two aspects of its meaning – love-making and the generation of new life – were to be wrenched apart. Deliberately separate the unitive from the procreative purpose of sexuality, and the possibility opens up for the legitimacy of any kind of sexual activity that fosters love, even outside of marriage. So for me the integrity of marriage was at the heart of the teaching.

I sometimes wonder if the Church might have come to a different view if Pope Paul hadn't set up a special commission to look at the issue of contraception, and it had been left instead for all the bishops meeting at the Vatican Council to rule on it. I'm not sure they would have come to a different conclusion, but perhaps the teaching might have been framed in a different way.

I wrote some years later in a letter to *The Tablet* that I considered *Humanae Vitae* to be a prophetic document. Pope Paul's intention was not to crush the faithful in any way but to invite them to rediscover the act of love within marriage as something sacred, as part of God's plan for creation, a thing of reverence as well as joy. My letter concluded by saying: '*Humanae Vitae* is not the last word on the subject but true progress will be made, not by ignoring or belittling it, but by going forward from it.' *Humanae Vitae* is well worth re-reading today.

In the summer of 1970, after four years as secretary to Derek, he appointed me as parish priest to a very large parish in Southampton. I had barely begun to get to know and minister to the people of the parish before I became involved in wider issues. A Conference of European Priests had been established following meetings of National Conferences of Priests in most of the countries in Europe. With a certain amount of reluctance, Heenan agreed that there should also be a National Conference here in England and Wales. I was asked to join a small group of priests from different parts of the country to plan the meeting. The convenor was a Corkman, Monsignor Michael Buckley, and the conference was held at the pastoral centre he had established at Woodhall, near Wetherby in Yorkshire. It was the first time the National Conference of Priests had met and it generated considerable interest and a certain amount of nervousness among the bishops, some of whom were distinctly wary at what they thought was a sort of 'trade union for priests'. What sort of trouble might be stirred up? Would the delegates start to demand a married priesthood? There's nothing so alarming to a bishop than a priest with a bee in his bonnet.

After three days Mick Buckley had still not reported back to Heenan, who was starting to grow agitated. I rang David Norris, Heenan's secretary, and asked: 'Do you think the cardinal would like to see me?' Norris replied: 'He certainly would.' So I went in to Archbishop's House on my way back from Leeds. I was late, and hungry, because the train had been delayed, and I hadn't eaten since breakfast. Over a hastily cooked supper, Heenan asked me the names of the priests who were there, and what they had each said. He eagerly took it all in. In fact, while there had been a certain sense of frustration among the priests at the sluggish pace of implementation of the directives of the Vatican Council and a desire for a bolder and more imaginative leadership from the bishops, the meeting had passed by without major controversy.

As a result of this meeting, a few priests from England and Wales were elected to represent Britain at another European Conference of Priests to take place in Geneva after Easter in 1971. At the same time, Pope Paul had called a general assembly of the synod of bishops in Rome, with the theme 'The Ministerial Priesthood and Justice in the World', which was scheduled to meet in October 1971. I found myself participating in both events. At the meeting of priests in Switzerland the atmosphere was extremely tense. The unease and disgruntlement felt among some priests in England and Wales was experienced even more keenly in other parts of Europe, particularly in Holland, Germany and France. At the end of the conference two of the priests, a Spanish Jesuit and myself, were elected to bring the resolutions of the meeting to the cardinal who was presiding over the preparations for the forthcoming synod of bishops in Rome on the priesthood. What I had not told anyone at the meeting of priests in Switzerland was that I was also a member of the planning group for the general synod of bishops. This had happened because the organizers of the preparatory document for the synod had asked the presidents of bishops' conferences to send one or two priests to help them in their task, and Heenan had put me forward as one of the three priests from Europe. So I was in a very strange situation. I was responsible for making representations on behalf of the European Conference of Priests to the committee planning the synod of bishops in Rome, of which I was a member. It was all slightly disconcerting to say the least.

It wasn't my first involvement in a general synod of bishops. I remember when the bishops had assembled at the previous synod, in 1969, to discuss cooperation between the Holy See and bishops' conferences, the synod fathers thought it would be a good idea to have a session at which a priest from each country would speak to them about matters of particular concern to them. Heenan asked me if I would speak on behalf of the priests of England and Wales. I prepared a short address, in Latin, about the ideal size of a diocese, which was something I felt quite strongly about. When the day arrived and we were sitting in the synod hall, one priest after another rose to make a radical speech, some of which questioned the mandatory celibacy of the clergy. When it was my turn to address the synod, I delivered my rather tame remarks about the size of the area a bishop might be expected to cover, but then I had a rush of blood to the head. Instead of sitting down, I said – I can still hear myself saying it, in terrible Latin – 'Habeo unum, alterum punctum' ('I have another point'). I stumbled on, saying, still in execrable Latin, that I didn't think there should be a change to allow priests to marry, but perhaps the ordination of married men should be considered. I sat down to a deafening silence. I could see Heenan looking at me sympathetically from the front row.

In the summer of 1971 I was starting to enjoy my new parish, The Immaculate Conception, Portswood, Southampton, and I had a growing feeling that I was going to be happy there. I had a curate, and there was a good crowd at Mass, about 800, including quite a lot of young people from the university. But I was to be whisked away.

I think the main reason I became rector of the English College in Rome, the *Venerabile*, was because of Heenan. I'd had a pizza in the spring with Jack Brewer, who was about to step down as vice-rector, and I remember discussing the possible candidates for the next rector. The bishops were eventually given a shortlist of three, but my name wasn't on it. It was the cardinal, I'm almost sure, who put me up for the job. The news of my appointment came in a letter from Heenan in the August of that eventful year of 1971. It was a shock. I remember walking up and down a beach on a holiday resort in Ireland, asking myself if I was indeed capable of fulfilling this very important position. I flew back to England and went to see Cardinal Heenan at his country house in Hare Street, Hertfordshire, where he was staying.

The two of us had supper together, and talked late into the night. I was wanting to talk about the College and the challenges I would face there, and what his plans for it were, to get a sense of my brief. But all Heenan wanted to talk about were his problems with defecting priests and trouble-making theologians, stirring up doubts among the simple faithful.

Anyway, the die was cast. I sadly relinquished my parish and flew to Rome in September, first of all to attend the general synod of bishops as an Auditor and then to take up my new responsibility as Rector. It had, indeed, been an extraordinary year.

In those years after the Council, working closely with the indefatigable Derek Worlock and with Cardinal Heenan sharing with me the heartbreak and depression the turmoil was causing him, the metaphor of an English spring seemed to perfectly evoke the stormy renewal of the Church in England. No matter how bright the sunshine might be in the morning, it would never be wise to leave the house without an umbrella.

6

Return to Rome

As the Italian writer Silvio Negro said, '*Roma, non basta una vita*' – for Rome, a lifetime is not enough. There are other cities in Europe which captivate: the beauty of Paris, the romance of Venice, the artistic treasures of Florence, the grandeur of London. But only Rome has earned the title of the 'eternal city'; monarchs, popes, emperors and dictators might mingle in the dust but, like the Tiber, Rome flows endlessly on. There are surprises around every corner: a gaggle of children playing in a baroque fountain, or lines of washing strung across the windows of a medieval palazzo. Like good wine, she is to be sipped not gulped, so that the tempo and delights of the city can be enjoyed to the full. And now here I was, in the autumn of 1971, back at the English College on the Via Monserrato, where I had studied for the priesthood in the 1950s, this time as Rector. It was to be a demanding but exhilarating six years.

I was only in Rome a few months when my mother died; Ellen got cancer and she was dead within a month. It was desperately sad. I had been thinking how lovely it would be for her to come out to visit me in Rome. I was able to get home. Catherine was living with her; my brother Jim was there, and Pat, Brian and I said Mass together round her bedside. Pat, the eldest of Ellen's three priest sons, was the natural leader in the family since my father's death. He was sharp, a brilliant mimic, a wonderful speaker and the life and soul of many a party; his parishioners loved him. He could never resist a joke, even when sometimes it might have served him better if he had kept it to himself. There was a recklessness about him. He would have been a remarkable bishop. Pat died in 1991.

I was returning to the centre of what was becoming known as 'the runaway Church'. The complacent and perhaps rather rigid and self-righteous Catholic Church I had known as a student had been unsettled and cracked open by the second Vatican Council. It wasn't just that a new self-understanding had emerged, a new appreciation of the mission of the Church. It was that there was now a ferment of different understandings of the Church's role and destiny. Every conversation I had on my return to Rome, whether it was with students or professors or other seminary rectors, seemed to throw up a different interpretation of the meaning of the documents of the Council; everyone seemed to have their own take on what had happened at the Council and what it meant for the Church. Rome was in a state of turmoil.

All of this closely affected seminaries, not least the English College. There were some obvious, superficial changes. Seminarians no longer dressed in long black cassocks, except for special occasions; lectures at the Gregorian University were no longer in Latin but in Italian. But the greatest change was in the way in which students were to be prepared, or 'formed' as we say, for the priesthood. No longer was the seminary a place where the daily life of the student would be determined by a fixed system of rules. The student was now expected to take much more responsibility for the crucial matters which pertained to his formation, namely, prayer, study, human development and pastoral experience. They were treated, you might say, more like adults. This was partly because the young men training for the priesthood when I returned to Rome in the 1970s tended to be older than in my own day, when many of us were still in our late teens and straight from school or junior seminary. And it was partly because it was increasingly recognized that if the Church was to have mature and responsible priests, they would have to be treated as mature and responsible young men during their priestly training.

It was a new ecclesiastical world and I did not always find it easy to adapt, especially in my first couple of years. The rector of a Catholic seminary is a cross between a parish priest and the abbot of a monastery. Like a parish priest, the rector's role is to be friendly and supportive to his community, as well as being a spiritual father and administering the sacraments. At the same time, like an abbot, the rector has to set the direction for the community, to preside and to rule, and, when necessary, to discipline. Sometimes, he was expected to encourage, at other times to teach and even to scold. It was my first real experience of leadership, and I learnt a lot about myself. I came to recognize some of my strengths and some of my weaknesses.

For the most part I greatly enjoyed living with and for my students, watching them grow and flourish. Some are now teaching at seminaries, others are parish priests and a few are bishops; others went on to careers outside the priesthood, and some are married with families. I remember them all with great affection. As they say about politics, a week is a long time in a seminary. My task was to ensure that the human, spiritual, intellectual and pastoral formation we offered at the English College was of at least an adequate standard. I could not claim that the formation in my time lived up to all the requirements for seminary formation that were to be set out in *Pastores dabo vobis* ('I shall give you shepherds'), the apostolic exhortation on the formation of priests issued by John Paul II in 1992. We did our best. I say 'we' because I was greatly helped and supported by my staff, who taught me lessons in collegiality and in the art of leadership that I tried never to forget. Together, we lived with the students, prayed with them, encouraged them and enjoyed their company. Week by week we would talk about them, assessing their progress, and weighing what further help they needed if they would one day be candidates for the priestly office. We held the future of these young men in our hands. I found myself stretched as never before; it was the most demanding and the most rewarding of tasks. In some ways those years as Rector of the English College were the most enjoyable of my life.

When I arrived, there was a question mark over the College's future. There was a feeling among some of the bishops that they shouldn't be training students abroad, that priestly formation was better done at home. And it was being said by some that discipline at the *Venerabile* had grown lax. The previous rector was a good man, liked and respected by the students. He had led the College during a turbulent period, but the bishops did not always appreciate the difficult and demanding task of being a seminary rector in the years immediately following the Council. The word was going back to them that the English College had become somewhat *avant garde*, and they were were hesitating to send any students there, preferring to send them instead to one of the English seminaries. Heenan was looking for someone who could steady the ship. A safe pair of hands.

Things were looking a little rocky; without any income from student fees it would be very hard for the College to continue. It was down to fewer than forty students, from sixty or seventy. One of the first things I did was to go round all the bishops trying to drum up support. I knew that the seminary couldn't be the same as it was. We had to change. We decided that the students would be trusted more, given more

Grandfather Murphy-O'Connor and family. Cork, 1920.

The Murphy-O'Connor family.

The Murphy-O'Connor family home. Reading, 1947.

The English College rugby team. Rome, 1951.

Day of our audience with Pope Pius XII. Rome, 1951.

Cardinal Griffin, staff and students of the English College. Rome, 1950.

Ordination as Bishop of Arundel and Brighton, 1977.

Meeting Pope Paul VI after being appointed Bishop of Arundel and Brighton. Rome, 1977.

Working as secretary to Bishop Derek Worlock.

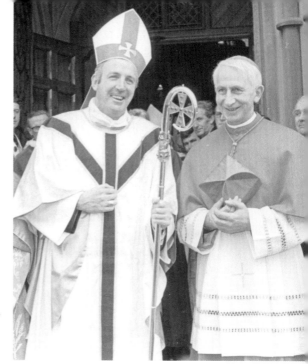

With Cardinal Basil Hume after being ordained as Bishop of Arundel and Brighton, 1977.

Meeting my young namesake after being ordained Bishop at Arundel cathedral, 1977.

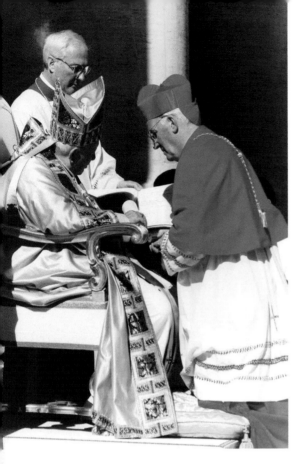

Being created cardinal by Pope John Paul II. Rome, 2001.

In conversation with Pope Benedict XVI.

A meeting of Pope Benedict and the secretariat of the synod of bishops.

In friendly conversation with the Archbishop of Canterbury, Rowan Williams.

On the golf course with Fr Edward Corbould and Archbishop Michael Bowen.

With Professor Henry Chadwick, a fellow member of ARCIC.

responsibility. I allowed the students to have their own keys, so they could let themselves in at night. This was the sort of thing some of the bishops didn't like.

On the whole the bishops would send their brighter students to the College, and sometimes, perhaps, the ones they were just a little frightened of, the ones with 'attitude'. They had a sort of hope that Rome would sort them out. But Rome was in a ferment. Everything seemed to be up for grabs. Some of the students thought that the rule of mandatory celibacy for priests, for example, was going to be changed. I can remember one priest, who had been at the English College, telling me: 'I was quite sure there would be a change in the celibacy rule, and I took my vows with that in mind.' While the students were pressing for more and more reforms, several of the bishops wanted me to turn back the clock, to go back to the old style. It's a position I've often found myself in – trying to broker a peace between the people who want to change everything and the people who want to change nothing.

The trick was to let the leash out gently, so that you could allow things to develop while staying in control. At the time, for example, women were not allowed in the dining room at the College. And of course the students were determined that this would be their next *cause célèbre*, the next barrier to be smashed in the march towards enlightenment. I wasn't unsympathetic. But when after a rugby match with a naval team, the senior student came to me and said, 'They've got their girlfriends with them, we'll invite them into the refectory for supper', I said, 'No. We have a rule, we must stick to it.' General outrage and disgust. 'And we thought this was a place of Christian hospitality', and all the rest of it. But I knew it wasn't a rule worth hanging on to. About a fortnight later, we had an Anglican bishop due to come for Sunday lunch. I told him that I would be delighted if his wife could come too. So the bishop turned up with his wife, something of a Mrs Proudie, wearing a large and impressive hat, and she processed into the refectory to general applause. Only a small thing. I'm not sure who won that one, but I felt I managed to implement changes in the College, without allowing things getting out of control.

Liturgy, of course, was another battleground. There were wrangles over whether Mass should be in Latin or in English, and over the quality of the liturgical texts; there were those who would want to stand when others would want to kneel, those who insisted on receiving communion in the hand and those who insisted it should be received on the tongue. 'What's the difference between a terrorist and a liturgist?' It's an old joke. Every rector and every bishop can supply the answer: 'You can negotiate with a terrorist.'

When I was training for the priesthood and when I was Rector, the issue of human development was not discussed or dealt with in any depth. In my student days we were not allowed to enter another student's room and we would go on walks or travel together in groups of three or more. It wouldn't be spelled out why. This was just the way things were done. When I was Rector, we discussed human formation with the students, but not as much as we should have done, and perhaps this left us vulnerable and unprepared for what was to come later. Sexual sins were discussed: adultery, of course, and incest too – but the sexual abuse of young people I don't think was ever mentioned. We were all committed to lives of chastity. Chastity was at the heart of our priesthood, which we understood as a giving of our whole lives to the service of the Lord and his people. Of course, this isn't always easy; for some, it can be a real struggle. We did not talk very much about the sexual orientation of students. Even in the 1970s, at least in Catholic seminaries, there was still a reserve, a reticence; perhaps we were naïve.

We hoped that the students would leave us emotionally mature, open and attentive to the people around them, capable of chaste, warm and affectionate friendships. But there's no doubt that the human formation of students was neglected to some extent in seminaries in my time, and this is a lesson that has been learnt at great cost.

There were often tussles with the bishops. Since they were, in effect, paying for the place, they had a tendency to try to do my job for me. I learnt how to keep them at arms' length, to keep control of the management of the College. It wasn't easy, but gradually I think we restored some discipline, without too many ructions, and the numbers started to creep up again. By the time I left, the College was in pretty good shape. The finances had recovered, and the student numbers were healthy. Since then, the College has been lucky with its rectors, and – although vocations to the priesthood are not as high as in previous decades – its future is secure. The rector of another seminary in Rome took me aside once. 'I feel like a matador', he told me. 'There are all these bulls charging at me – students, staff, bishops, accountants – and' – he did a little shimmy – 'I have to somehow skip to let them past and still keep my balance ...'. I knew the feeling. 'I only lasted two years', he added. I managed six. Not without problems, but all in all this time back in Rome was a formative and enjoyable experience.

My time as Rector was my first experience of running something, of being in authority. It was something of a launch into the deep. I was determined I would lead the College in my own way. I found that I was good at managing people. I wasn't a great teacher or academic, but I had a gift for working with others to create a community where people could rub along together, and pray together and flourish together. I loved to encourage the young, to bring out the best in the students. That was the most satisfying thing. I enjoyed creating a place of hospitality, where guests would be welcomed and enjoyed. I knew my own short-comings, and didn't mind asking for help. I could stay calm in a crisis. And I found that I was a pretty good negotiator and deal-maker. I was a natural ecumenist.

Because of its long history, there are certain duties that go with being the Rector of the English College, and I found myself expected to play a certain role in the life of the Church in Rome. In some ways, the College is a sort of mix between embassy and hotel, and the Rector is at the same time an unofficial ambassador and an unpaid concierge. English bishops would regularly roll up and I would be expected to act as host and go-between in their relationship with the officials of the Roman curia – the bureaucrats and administrators who take care of the business of the Church.

I was also responsible for our relationship with the Jesuit-run university which my students attended for their studies, the Gregorian. For a time I was chairman of the rectors of all the seminaries and colleges in Rome and we used to have regular meetings to discuss matters that pertained to the studies of the students. In my own student days, most of the students were straight from school or junior seminary, and we were often still in our late teens when we arrived. By the 1970s, when I returned to Rome, students had, for the most part, already studied at university before being sent to Rome to prepare for the priesthood. They just couldn't face traipsing over to the Greg every morning to listen to lectures, with no opportunity for discussion or interaction. One day, the rector of the American College and I went to see Pedro Arrupe, the much-admired superior general of the Jesuits, to see if we could persuade him to improve the format of the teaching programme. We didn't have much success.

Another aspect of the life of the rector was to play host to a great number of visitors to the College. I was never allowed to forget that the origins of the *Venerabile* were as a 'hospice', a place of accommodation for English pilgrims in Rome before the Reformation. The late Leonard Cheshire came to lunch a number of times. Group Captain Cheshire had been a highly decorated RAF pilot in the Second World War, though he was to resign from the RAF after serving as an observer of the dropping of the nuclear bomb on Nagasaki. He was someone I greatly admired for his work for disabled people and for setting up the Cheshire Homes, now a major worldwide charity. He was a deeply spiritual man and the conversation over lunch would be of heavenly rather than earthly matters. In my view, he was one of the greatest Englishmen of the twentieth century.

Another visitor was Harold Macmillan, then long retired from the premiership. During lunch, an American priest began to criticize President Nixon, who had just resigned at the height of the Watergate affair. I asked Macmillan what he thought of it all. He gave that familiar droop of the eyes and said: 'I felt rather sorry for him. I just thought he was a fool to bug himself.' He gave a magnificent speech to the student body at the end of lunch. Muriel Spark, who lived in Rome at that time, also came to lunch. She invited the students to suggest a dramatic title for her next novel. Later, during one of the many interminable Italian postal strikes, she asked someone at the College to pack the typescript of her next novel with him when he flew back to London, so it could be delivered to her publisher. Its title was *The Abbess of Crewe*.

Norman St John-Stevas, the Conservative MP, was another regular. Norman always had an eye for *objets d'art*. He once asked me if he could take away a rather good bust of Pope Pius IX and when I demurred, he offered to swap it for his complete works of Walter Bagehot. The deal was agreed on the condition that the bust would be returned to the College after his death. Norman was a bit of a card, but always very enjoyable company. Among the many cardinals who came to lunch was the Archbishop of Kraków, one Karol Wojtyla. Afterwards, he made a dramatic speech to the students and I remember thinking to myself, 'Here is somebody to watch!' This wasn't my first experience of Cardinal Wojtyla. When I'd been in Rome with Cardinal Heenan for the 1971 synod, Wojtyla had invited all the English-speaking bishops who were present in Rome to come to the Polish Centre for a reception. After about half an hour, we heard this strong baritone voice ringing out with a Polish song, and then all the Polish prelates present joined in eagerly. It was, of course, Cardinal Wojtyla. After their second song I said to Heenan that maybe the English-speaking prelates should sing a song too. Among the American, Canadian, Irish and Indian bishops present it was difficult to come up with a song we all knew well enough to join in. Eventually we began to sing, very badly, 'The Rose of Tralee'. Cardinal Wojtyla looked less than impressed. He soon launched into another Polish favourite.

During my period of office as Rector, I agreed that we would take two Anglican ordinands for a term as students at the College, an arrangement that has continued. Of course I had to clear the idea with Heenan. 'Look,' I said, 'I've been offered a couple of Anglican students. Would you mind if I accepted them?' There was a sort of wry despair about Heenan towards the end. 'Of course, Cormac,' he joked, 'and why not take in a couple of hottentots to study with you while you're at it.' In return, I sent two students to study at Westcott, the Anglican training college in Cambridge.

Another notable visitor was the distinguished missiologist and minister of the United Reformed Church, Norman Goodall, who was giving a course of lectures at the Greg. He was a wonderful man and I greatly enjoyed his company. He was later to write: 'My residence at the *Venerabile* proved to be a period of deep renewal of my own faith as well as one in which I was wonderfully blessed by the friendship of students and faculty.' Although I met Norman again once or twice after his first visit, we lost touch for many years, but it just happened that ten years later, after I had returned to England, I called to see him at Oxford, just before his death. We spoke together, we blessed each other and I was happy that our friendship had continued and had ended in such a providential way.

In April 1977 we played host to Donald Coggan, the Archbishop of Canterbury, who had come to Rome for a meeting with Pope Paul VI. Coggan was a very welcome guest, though his visit was not without incident. On the evening before his audience with the pope, the archbishop, who belonged to the evangelical wing of the Church of England, preached a sermon in the American Episcopal church of St Paul's, in the via Napoli. It was reported that Coggan had rather hamfistedly called for indiscriminate intercommunion between Anglicans and Catholics, playing into the hands of conservatives in the curia who like nothing better than evidence that the ecumenical movement was dangerously flirting with the idea that one religion was as good as another. In fairness to Coggan, his remarks, if somewhat provocative, had been altogether more modest. He was not an advocate of so-called 'wild-cat' intercommunion (*l'intercommunion sauvage*). I have learnt over the years that in the search for the unity of Christians, grand gestures have to be measured out with great economy. Ecumenism tends to be a dogged progression from one almost imperceptible nuance to another.

However, a call came through to the English College that the Vatican was not happy with the draft of the joint declaration the pope and the archbishop were due to sign the following day in the Sistine Chapel.

Someone, it was suspected, had used the text of Coggan's sermon to make trouble. So at 9 a.m. the next morning, with the declaration due to be signed in a few hours, there was a meeting at the College between Archbishop Coggan and his aide, Edward Knapp-Fisher, and Cardinal Jan Willebrands and Bishop Ramón Torrella Cascante of the Secretariat for Christian Unity to look at the proposed changes to the agreed text. They decided they would challenge the changes. Torrella Cascante would make the call to Mgr Giovanni Benelli, the *sostituto*. Unfortunately, the College telephone exchange chose this moment to break down. Torrella Cascante went out and telephoned Benelli from a bar next door. The comments on the changes were largely accepted without fuss. The duplicating machine at the secretariat was set to work to produce 2,000 copies of the finally agreed statement. The Coggan party was sped through the streets of Rome with a police escort to meet their 12 o'clock deadline. I tootled along behind in my battered old car. With a few minor titivations, the Common Declaration was signed in the Sistine Chapel. No wonder Willebrands was a bit flustered when the party returned to the College. While Coggan was giving his press conference, I sat down with the Dutchman in my office and said to him: 'Your Eminence, what you need is a stiff gin and tonic.' He nodded gratefully.

Willebrands was a lovely man. It is said that when two Italians knocked each other out in the conclave after the death of Pope John Paul I, the cardinals seriously considered this Dutch cardinal before they turned to the Pole, Wojtyla. Willebrands taught me a lot about how to be truly ecumenical. It is about meeting people – really meeting people. You don't go for the jugular, or search for what you think is the weak point in the other's position. You look instead for common ground; start with what you agree with, and then move on to the areas of difference. I was beginning to learn that ecumenism was not 'you-come-in-ism'. It was about a sharing of gifts.

Cardinal John Carmel Heenan died on 7 November 1975, aged 70, and I flew back to London to attend his funeral. I had been close to the cardinal for the previous nine years and I had great admiration and affection for him. Although his death came quite suddenly, he had already indicated that he wished to step down as Archbishop of Westminster on grounds of health and the apostolic delegate, Archbishop Bruno Heim, had already been taking soundings as to who should be his successor. As is normal, rumours abounded. Was it to be my old boss, Derek Worlock, Bishop of Portsmouth, a front-runner in the eyes of many in Rome? Or was it to be Gordon Wheeler of Leeds, or George Patrick Dwyer of Birmingham? Basil Hume's name had first appeared in connection with the post in September 1975, in a *Sunday Times* article that had run the rule over several possible contenders, but he was very much a dark horse.

In my recollection, this is what happened. Dwyer and Wheeler ruled themselves out of the running, Dwyer because he had already been Bishop of Leeds and then of Birmingham and did not feel able to accept another diocese, and Bishop Wheeler because of a heart attack he had suffered a few years earlier. This left Derek – but there was considerable opposition to his appointment among some of the clergy in Westminster, several of whom made their feelings known to the nuncio. So the field was left open. Bruno Heim said he received almost a thousand letters from people from all over England and Wales, many of them indicating that a new style of leadership was needed for the Catholic Church in Westminster and in the country as a whole. The only bishops who knew Basil well were Gordon Wheeler and John McClean of Middlesbrough, both of whom had made regular visits to Ampleforth and both of whom were great admirers of its abbot. Wheeler pressed his candidature with the nuncio, with the help of old Amplefordians such as the 17th Duke of Norfolk and the journalist Hugo Young. The abbot primate of the Benedictine Confederation, Rembert Weakland, later to be Archbishop of Milwaukee, was another acting behind the scenes, and the nuncio himself sometimes said that the recommendation of Archbishop of Canterbury Donald Coggan had been decisive.

Pope Paul VI duly appointed Basil Hume as Archbishop of Westminster on 9 February 1976. It was an inspired appointment and greatly welcomed by everyone. A week before it was announced, Derek Worlock was appointed Archbishop of Liverpool, where he was to be a great success, especially in his ecumenical cooperation with the Anglican Bishop of Liverpool, David Sheppard, and the Methodist leader, John Newton. Within a few days, the archbishop-designate came to Rome and stayed at the English College. Basil was anxious and uncertain as to whether he could cope with his new office. After all, he had never been a parish priest or a bishop and had been a monk at Ampleforth or at houses of study for over forty years. I recall driving him to the Vatican for an audience with the Holy Father in the papal apartments. They spoke easily together in French. Basil came back to the College a changed man. Pope Paul had fulfilled, as he did to countless other bishops, the task given by the Lord to St Peter, 'Confirm your brethren'. He told Basil not to be concerned and that he should continue to have pastoral care of his new Archdiocese in the light of his Benedictine spirituality and that he should have no fear. His final words to Basil were to stay with him throughout all his years in Westminster: 'Always remain a monk.'

A few months later when Basil was created a cardinal, he stayed again at the College, and we had another audience with Pope Paul in his apartments. I remember the pope saying to me, with a smile: 'Long time no see!' My one-to-one meetings with Pope Paul were always quite intimate, personal exchanges. Paul would always look at me face to face. His eyes would meet mine. He had real warmth. Pope Paul suffered a lot. These were years of great difficulty for the Church, and he felt it keenly. It just wasn't possible for Pope Paul to implement the Council, and I think he knew it. There were just too many counter-currents for him to push through all the reforms it called for.

Pope Paul was followed by a pope who, in some ways, closed the windows that Pope John had opened. This allowed the storms to subside – for the ideas of the Council not to be lost, but to be set in aspic for a while. I don't think Pope John Paul reversed the work of the Council; indeed, in some ways he developed it. Who can forget his tireless visiting of the local churches around the world, and his meetings with other Christian leaders and the leaders of other faiths, culminating in his invitation to them to join him in praying for peace at Assisi in 1986? And we should also remember his remarkable encyclical letter of 1995, *Ut unum sint* ('That they may be one') in which he asked fellow Christians and Church leaders and theologians to help him discover how to exercise his ministry in a way that would carry forward our commitment to Christian unity and common witness. Some have said that we need a third Vatican Council. Pope Francis has said 'No'. He's right. Instead, after a period of the finger perhaps hovering over the 'Pause' button I think he is pressing 'Play'. It is time for the Council to be implemented at last.

I met Cardinal Hume many times during the next two years, as he was often in Rome on business and always stayed with us at the English College. He greatly enjoyed the company of the students and they were delighted to have easy contact with such a friendly and kind bishop. He was a great support and help to me personally during my final years as Rector. In October 1976, Cyril Cowderoy, the Archbishop of Southwark, died and the following March the Bishop of Arundel and Brighton, my friend Michael Bowen, succeeded him. I remember Hervé Carrier, the French Canadian rector of the Greg, saying to me after I had come back to Rome after Heenan's funeral: 'Cormac, you'll be a bishop soon.' Nuncios often send round questionnaires, so I had a good idea that my name had gone forward for another diocese before Arundel and Brighton came up. So when in November of 1977 I was called into the office of the Cardinal in charge of the appointment of bishops to be told that Pope Paul wished me to have pastoral care of the diocese of Arundel and Brighton, it was a surprise, but not a complete shock. I was 45 years old and a new life awaited me.

7

Batting for Arundel and Brighton

Although I would have been happy enough to have remained at the English College for a few more years, some people had indicated that I might be considered for a diocese, so I was not totally unprepared when I was called to the offices of the Congregation for Bishops and was told by the Cardinal Prefect that Pope Paul wished me to have the pastoral care of the diocese of Arundel and Brighton.

After a retreat at Quarr Abbey on the Isle of Wight I was ordained bishop in Arundel Cathedral on 21 December 1977. I was only the third bishop of the diocese, which had been created out of the archdiocese of Southwark in 1965. Arundel and Brighton covers the counties of Sussex and Surrey. Sussex is somewhat rural, and has a long coastline stretching from Chichester to Rye, with Brighton at its centre; Surrey is for the most part suburbia, with commuters from towns like Weybridge and Woking travelling into London every day.

What is a bishop for? And what does he actually do? I saw my main task as the pastoral care of the people of the diocese, and I immediately set out to visit to each one of the 115 parishes and to meet all the priests of the diocese. It took me three or four years to get round to every parish. I would go on a Sunday, offer one Mass and preach at the other Masses, meet with the parish council and greet as many of the parishioners as I could. In the early years I often stayed overnight and visited the parish primary school the next morning.

Always at the front of my mind was that I had to help my brother priests serve the people of God. They were my co-workers, presiding at Mass, absolving sinners, anointing the sick, proclaiming and explaining the Gospel, and caring for the people in their parish. Every Friday I invited three priests of the diocese to join me for a chat and a modest meal. I knew from my own experience that the life of a priest can be very tough, and it is not unusual for priests to face loneliness, depression and burnout. One of the first things I learnt as a bishop was the importance of making time to listen to my priests. We would focus on their prayer life and their pastoral work in the parish, and I would try to make sure they were looking after themselves, eating properly and getting some exercise and taking holidays.

The parish visits would also give me an opportunity to spend time with the priest. Some of the visits had unintended results. In one parish, the priest had a young puppy with sharp teeth, and during the night the dog chewed my new overcoat which I had left on a chair. The following Sunday the parish priest led his dog on a leash to the sanctuary, and explained to the people what had happened. He then indicated the message hanging round the dog's neck: *I am a repentant sinner*.

I organized a number of in-service training days for priests, responding to the Vatican Council's call for the continued professional development of priests in the years after their ordination. Our theology and knowledge of scripture might have grown rusty since our days in seminary, and these were good opportunities for study and prayer. Most importantly, we kept abreast of new resources and best practice in the celebration of the liturgy, which we all saw as at the heart of our vocation as priests.

The priests of the diocese had already undertaken something called the Ministry to Priests programme; as a result many of the priests had a mentor or spiritual director to guide and support them, and there were several groups of priests who met together once a month for exercise and fellowship. When the founder of the Ministry to Priests programme agreed to come from the USA to give a retreat to all the priests of the diocese, I urged everyone to attend. At the last moment, our speaker pulled out, but assured me that he would send another American priest to give the retreat in his place, who would be just as good. The substitute retreat-giver turned out to be a disaster. The conferences were dull and banal, and I could see that the clergy were becoming restless. I had visions of no one turning up for the second session. I decided to continue the retreat myself. I remember driving back to my house and rather desperately unearthing notes of previous retreats I had given. The next morning, I explained to the clergy that there had been a change of plan. On the whole, I think they were relieved; even if they might not have held out high hopes for my retreat, they felt that even their bishop could not be worse than what they had suffered so far. It was the first time I had ever given a retreat to my own clergy and, thank God, it didn't go too badly.

I was always keenly aware of the priestly office of the bishop, which is to lead the diocese in its most important function: the celebration of the liturgy. In the words of the Vatican Council: 'The bishop is the steward of the grace and the supreme priesthood, above all in the Eucharist, which he himself offers, or insures that it is offered, from which the Church ever derives its life on which it thrives' (*Lumen Gentium*, 26). A very important preoccupation of mine was not only to ensure that the people were able to participate in the celebration of Mass every Sunday but to ensure that the Mass was celebrated worthily, reverently and with the full participation of the faithful.

It was also part of my role to teach and proclaim the faith of the Church and the Good News of the Gospel. Bishops regularly write pastoral letters which are usually read out at all Masses on a particular Sunday in the liturgical year. I was among the first of the bishops to send a recording of their pastoral letter to the parishes, so that the people were able to hear my voice proclaiming the message. So long as the public address system was good, this was very successful. Often when I visited a parish, people would say that it was good to meet 'the face behind the voice'.

The prayer life of a diocese is crucial, and this includes both communal and private prayer. I was always uncomfortably conscious that this assumed that I myself was a man of prayer, and I often had to examine my conscience as to the time I gave to the practice of the presence of God in my own personal life. Perhaps this is the most important thing about a bishop – that he is a person of prayer. What a bishop does is important – but what matters more is what he is.

As I look back over my life, I see how preoccupied I have always been by the idea of 'family'. I might sometimes idealize the family – I know, of course, that families can sometimes be places of loneliness and fear and abuse. My own family background was loving and secure, and no doubt this is why my favourite image of the Church has always been that of a family – one might think of the Church as 'the family of God'. As a young priest, I'd been inspired by Yves Congar's book *Lay People in the Church*. 'Many of our contemporaries', he pointed out, 'find that sometimes the very institution of the Church is a barrier, obscuring her deep and living mystery which they can find, or find again, only from below, through little Church cells where the Mystery is lived directly and with great simplicity.' This rang true to me. People often mistrust big institutions, whether they are banks, political parties or churches. But in small groups, people meet other people face to face. Church is experienced not as a faceless institution but as a community, a family, to whose life all its members contribute; a space where we meet as friends, as followers of the Gospel, to pool our resources, material and spiritual. The creation of small communities had been the most satisfying experience of my life as an assistant priest, and now that I was a bishop, one of the things I wanted to do was to see how far the idea of the Church as 'the family of God' could be lived out and made real in the life of a diocese.

Over the years I launched a host of programmes aimed at grass-roots renewal. Perhaps the boldest was my decision to adopt the 'Renew' programme, which had been initiated in the United States. After paying a visit to the USA to find out the implications and practicalities, I announced it to the diocese. From 1988 to 1990, we devoted most of our resources to the programme, which I asked a very competent and inspirational priest, Kevin McHugh, assisted by Sr Hazel Buckley FMDM, to direct. During Lent and then a six-week period in late autumn, parishes were invited to nourish a deeper faith by prayer and a closer relationship to Christ, and to become more authentic witnesses to him in daily life. Materials, events, and especially development of faith-sharing communities were all directed towards this end. In their meetings, the groups would have a time for prayer, reading a passage of scripture and the discussion of practical ways to deepen their understanding of Catholic faith and the mission of the Church.

There were passionate disagreements about how the diocese should approach justice and peace issues. I didn't mind – it seems natural to me that people will disagree about how we should relate as Catholics to social issues. Some were critical of me for adopting this form of renewal without proper consultation. I have to confess it probably was a bit 'top-down'. There were some priests in the diocese who had no trouble containing their enthusiasm for the Renew process and I knew if I didn't push it through it wouldn't have happened at all. Sometimes even a bishop has to stick his head over the parapet and take a lead. As Machiavelli pointed out, 'there is nothing more difficult to carry out, nor more doubtful of success, nor more dangerous to handle, than to initiate a new order of things. For the reformer has enemies in all those who profit by the old order, and only lukewarm defenders in all those who would profit by the new order.'

A glass is half full or half empty. The success of the Renew programme depended for the most part on the enthusiasm and leadership of the parish priests. Renew had mixed results, but I think we went some way to recapturing the basic concept of Christian community. There was a renewal of a sense of service to those in need and, through fellowship with other Christians, I think there were a few who quietly found the courage to become radical witnesses to society of Gospel values.

The cathedral of the diocese was in Arundel, the seat of the Duke of Norfolk, whose ancestor had paid for the church to be built in the nineteenth century. It's a fine building but in a slightly remote location. I was determined to find ways to encourage as many people as possible to come there for events and celebrations, and it gradually became the centre of the life of the diocese.

The Duke was Miles Fitzalan-Howard, who had had a distinguished career in the Army before inheriting the title in 1975. Miles could be bluff and plain-speaking but he was to prove a loyal friend and a great support. His predecessor, Bernard, the 16th Duke, had been in office for almost sixty years and together with his wife, Lavinia, had been a benevolent presence in Arundel and, indeed, in the county for all that time. It was not easy for Miles, who was a distant cousin, to take over, but he gradually won people's respect and affection.

I lived in a beautiful house in Storrington, a village about six miles from Arundel. As well as a priest-secretary, three Franciscan Sisters also lived in, taking care of the household with great love and devotion. We were a small community and that was important to me. I was always up early. We had a chapel at the top of the house so I'd be up there and we'd say morning and evening prayer together, and then we'd have some time for private prayer. We were able to use the large house for all kinds of gatherings. Every year, for example, we opened up the house to disabled people and their families. There'd be 500 or so of us. After an open-air Mass and confirmations in the garden, there would be tea for everyone and then a dance. One father would come regularly with his disabled daughter. When they danced I couldn't help noticing the expression on his face, a look of great pain and great love. The depth of his love for his daughter deepened his anguish, and, in a mysterious way, it was as if the suffering only deepened the love. I learned so much about the human heart from my meetings with these extraordinary young people and their parents and carers.

I was also able to use the house to hold occasional meetings with doctors from the diocese. Having come from a medical family, I always had a certain sympathy for Catholic doctors who had to face many new challenges in their professional life and it was good to give them an opportunity to talk, together with one or two priests, about their life and work. I was also able to have regular meetings with young people. In my early years as bishop, once a month about sixty young people would come from different parishes, and we would chat, have a period of prayer, followed by a bowl of soup together. I enjoyed these evenings immensely and they were very helpful not only for them, but, perhaps even more so, for myself.

When I think of young people, I am reminded of the annual diocesan pilgrimage to Lourdes. Every year at the end of July, after the schools had broken up, about 800 of us would set off on the journey: doctors, nurses, over a hundred sick and disabled people, and about two or three hundred young people, most of whom would be studying at one of the Catholic schools in the diocese or be starting at university. Coaches picked up people and their luggage from points all over the diocese and brought them all to Newhaven. We'd board a cross-Channel ferry to Calais, where there'd be a train waiting for us, then we'd travel together through the night, arriving into Lourdes the following morning. It was all extraordinarily well organized by Lady Sarah Clutton, the daughter of Bernard, the 16th Duke.

There was always a great sense of adventure and excitement, especially among the young people, the *brancardiers* and *handmaids*, whose job was to look after the sick and minister to them during the five or six days sojourn in Lourdes. They would be involved immediately, eagerly helping the sick and disabled and their bags onto the train, and racing up and down the corridors between the carriages. When we arrived we would split up into groups of sixty or so, each group staying in one of the hotels around the town. The pilgrims who needed specialist care stayed in the Accueil, a purpose-built facility that offered medical help twenty-four hours a day. We would all be buoyed by the cheerfulness and faithfulness of the sick.

For some of the youngsters, it was the first time they had travelled abroad without their parents. The processions and the visits to the baths and the grotto, the trips to the shops and cafés, were all a terrific adventure. In the evenings, of course, they'd sneak out for a drink, and we used to have to go round the restaurants and bars rounding them up. On the last night we'd have a Mass just for the young people and the helpers, and I would give a little homily. The combination of caring for the sick, of prayer and devout celebration of the Mass, as well as the enjoyment of each other's company, often had a profound effect. For many of them, it was their first real taste of the Christian life.

The experience each year of living for a few days in a community where we prayed together and helped each other and enjoyed each other – young people, their teachers, the doctors and nurses, the priests and the bishop, and at the centre of it all the sick and the disabled – always refreshed my faith and revived my drooping spirits.

It was my job to ensure that every parish is taken good care of, and this involved the delicate and sensitive task of arranging the clergy of the diocese so that, so far as possible, square pegs were not put into round holes. When I arrived in the diocese there were about 140 priests to be allocated to 115 parishes. Moving a priest from parish to parish is a very sensitive task and I used to spend a lot of time talking to priests about possible moves and trying to ensure that they were content with their posting. I often tell the story of the parish priest who told his parishioners one Sunday: 'I have some bad news for you. I've been told by the bishop that I am to be moved to another parish. But, don't worry, the bishop has assured me that he is sending a good man in my place.' After Mass the parish priest went outside and he saw two elderly ladies in tears. 'Don't cry,' he told them, 'I know you're sad, but don't forget the bishop has said that he would send a good priest in my place.' One of the ladies looked up and said: 'But Father, he said that last time.'

In my view, an assistant priest should stay in a parish for between three and five years, and between seven to twelve years is long enough for a parish priest to be in one place. Although they were never formally announced, these guidelines became known and understood in the diocese. They gave both the priests and myself a certain flexibility about the timing, but they meant that moves never became a bolt from the blue. I think the priests knew what was in my mind and, on the whole, were content to move after a good number of years in a particular parish.

There are horses for courses. Some liked Surrey, some preferred Sussex. And some were better on their own, so you'd put them somewhere where they wouldn't have a curate. With the advice of a small group of priests I shuffled the pack as fairly as I could. I was lucky. I had a devoted and friendly group of priests. There were a few rows, but on the whole we cooperated well to ensure that the mission of the Church was fulfilled with all the faithfulness and courage we could muster.

I was ultimately responsible for the training of students for the priesthood, for the welfare of sick and retired priests, for the building or repair of the schools, and many other projects which are part of the life of the diocese. The diocese controlled significant assets and there was always some concern about whether we would have sufficient income to cover our expenditure. I must confess I have never lost sleep over money. My strategy, if you could call it that, was to pray and to trust that the Lord would provide – and then to be sure to recruit a professional and reliable group of men and women to act as trustees of the resources of the diocese, and to hand over day-to-day responsibility for management and administration to them. I was fortunate to be assisted by many kind and very able people, including Terence Stonehill, the financial secretary.

The sixty primary and eleven Catholic secondary schools in the diocese were very much part of my concern. The crucial thing is to find good head teachers, and we got that right more often than not. If there is a good head there is a good school – and vice versa. On the whole, our primary schools had an excellent reputation, as they do all over the country, and made up a significant portion of the education provided in Sussex and Surrey. One or two of the secondary schools I was a bit more worried about. It's very difficult to be a successful head of a Catholic secondary school – it takes passion, imagination and administrative ability. People like that aren't easy to find.

The Vatican Council set up new structures for consultation for every diocese in the worldwide Church. There was to be a council of priests, consultors, a diocesan pastoral council, and various other means for involving lay people in the government of the diocese. It's pretty complicated. The diocesan council, a large body of lay people with some priests, came together once a year to discuss and to comment on various aspects of the mission and work of the diocese. These structures have their uses, but I found that meetings with lay people individually or in small groups were sometimes more helpful than these larger meetings. I found the most helpful consultation body, apart from conversations with my vicars general, was the deans of the diocese. The diocese was divided into twelve deaneries, each with a dean, elected by the priests and then appointed by the bishop. My meetings with the deans were always extremely helpful. They knew better than anyone what was going on in the parishes, where there was a problem or where there was someone who needed help. And I was able to talk over my plans and ideas for the diocese, knowing I would get honest and well-informed feedback. I was blessed by good priests and, gradually, a number of permanent deacons and lay men and women.

I was lucky, too, in the religious of the diocese, who were a powerful witness to a life of prayer and dedication to an evangelical life. When

I arrived in the diocese there were over ninety convents and I was always happy to meet with so many good nuns, always open to offer cooperation and help in whatever part of the diocese they were in. I was also fortunate to have a Benedictine monastery and school in the diocese, at Worth Abbey, near Crawley. The Abbey is a place of welcome and encouragement for everyone, Catholic or not, seeking a closer relationship with God. It is a precious place of silent prayer and reflection, where it is also possible to follow the rhythm of the monastic day, structured around the community's prayer and liturgy. The Abbey is at the heart of the diocese. The monks and the other men religious of the diocese became an integral part of my life, and their teaching, preaching and pastoral care was much valued by everyone.

When I arrived in Arundel in December 1977, James Callaghan was Prime Minister; by the time I left, Margaret Thatcher and John Major had come and gone and the Labour Party was back in power, with Tony Blair riding high. During the years I served as bishop, the majority of people in Sussex and Surrey saw growing comfort and prosperity. Yet while material conditions certainly improved, in many ways the quality of our lives coarsened. The acquisition of wealth does not necessarily bring fulfilment to the human heart, or automatically produce a civilized society. We had a partnership with a diocese in Peru, Chulucanas, and I visited Peru several times, usually staying with one of the Arundel priests serving there. It was a long way from Arundel. I do not want to idealize communities wrestling with poverty, lack of opportunity and very serious social problems. But the people I met in Peru displayed, amid the simplicity of their lives, an extraordinary contentment and sense of thankfulness, not least for their faith. Too much money can cripple joy and freedom. In greedily grasping at material things, we can become enslaved by them – the very opposite of the liberation and fulfilment for which the human heart longs.

The first time I went to Chulucanas, my priest-secretary Jeremy Lear came with me. I would often say, 'we are all one human family', and I was a keen supporter of Cafod's work to end poverty and injustice in developing countries. But meeting my brothers and sisters from poor communities in the flesh really brought the urgency of the Church's 'preferential option for the poor' home to me for the first time. A few years later, Jeremy asked to serve in our sister diocese in Peru. Later I went to stay with him, and I could see that although he had always loved his life as a priest in the diocese, and lived it to the full, he was never happier than he was now, living and serving among the poorest of the poor. Not long after I returned home, Jeremy was killed when the car he was travelling in went off the road. Another priest, a Peruvian, was also killed and the other two occupants of the car, also Peruvian priests, were injured. Jeremy was 35. I flew to Chulucanas for the funeral. I felt a very personal sense of sadness and loss at Jeremy's death. He was my first secretary, and had been a dear friend to me. We would often take the household's dog for long walks on the Downs. He was gentle and kind, and his firmness of faith made him a most attractive personality.

I cannot finish this chapter without mentioning some of the people who were particularly close to me during those years. There were my priest-secretaries, first Jeremy, then Benny O'Shea, Ken Freeman – who also died at an early age and is sorely missed – Kieron O'Brien, Tom Treherne, Tony Barry and Kevin Dring. They were all very kind to me and a great help, as was my friend Barry Wymes. I have already mentioned the sisters who were my friends and who cared for me and the household with such graciousness and attention to detail. They were the angels of Storrington. But I must particularly mention

Sr Damian McGrath. Damian has been a secretary to me for over thirty years and has done a great service, not only to me personally but also to the priests and people of two dioceses. All these companions and friends have nodded politely whenever Cormac has come up with his latest 'idea', and all have heard Cormac's familiar stories many times without complaint, although they have stopped pretending that they haven't heard them before. But Damian has suffered the most. I am enormously grateful to her for her devoted service and patient friendship.

Perhaps I became increasingly focused on the diocese at the expense of wider concerns. The English and Welsh bishops tended to leave national and international affairs to Basil and Derek. Our task was to take care of things at a local level. One reason why my work on the Anglican-Roman Catholic International Commission, which began in 1982, was so important to me was that for a few weeks every year it took me out of diocesan affairs, which can become all-consuming.

Once or twice I think my name was mentioned for a move to another diocese. George Patrick Dwyer told me that he was very annoyed that I'd been made the Bishop of Arundel and Brighton. 'I wanted you to wait another three years at the English College and then take over from me in Birmingham.' George Patrick thought the rugged industrial landscape of the West Midlands would have suited my gifts more than the well-manicured golf courses of Rye and Walton Heath. When Birmingham did come up, I'd only been in Arundel a couple of years, and the Duke might have leaned on Basil to keep me in Storrington; but you can never be sure how these decisions are made. A joke doing the rounds at the time suggested that the apostolic nuncio who advised the pope on the appointment must have thought that Couve de Murville was French for Cormac

Murphy-O'Connor. Later, Basil told me he would like me to go to Wales because he wanted me on the small council of five archbishops who formed a sort of inner cabinet of advisors. Lord Longford came to stay with me when he was writing a book about bishops. He rang me up later to say: 'I've put your name forward to be the next Archbishop of Cardiff.' That was nice of him, but I was happy where I was. I had another call a week later. This time, he said: 'Cormac, I've been talking to a Peer from Wales, he thinks they must have a Welshman, and so I don't think I can put you forward after all.' I'm not sure Lord Longford had a decisive influence in these matters, but Wales was to get a native Welshman as its archbishop. I don't think my name was in the frame for a move after that. When Derek died in 1997, I thought perhaps I might be considered for Liverpool, along with David Konstant and Vincent Nichols. In fact, none of us were being mentioned at all, and eventually Pat Kelly was appointed.

For the last five years, I knew in my heart that I had been in the diocese long enough. Here I was moving priests around after ten or twelve years to stop them getting stale, and I'd been in Arundel for twenty. It wasn't so much that I was tired. I just felt I'd given it what I could and that the diocese needed a change. I'd formed a plan in my mind to hold a synod in the year 2002. It would be the diocese's first-ever synod, and I intended to give lay people together with the bishop and the priests of the diocese a chance to decide the shape of things to come. I had also decided that I would ask the pope if at the conclusion of the synod I could step down as bishop. I would be 70, and bishop of the same diocese for twenty-five years. I wasn't quite sure what I wanted to do, perhaps to retire to live in a parish, where I could help out with saying Mass and hearing confessions. It was to be nearly ten years more before I could realize that ambition.

Perhaps now I look at these years through rose-tinted spectacles, because being a bishop in Arundel and Brighton was so different from the turbulent years that followed in Westminster. But Arundel and Brighton will always be a place of wonder in my imagination. I have so many fond memories. On a Bank Holiday Monday in 1990 we celebrated the silver jubilee of the establishment of the diocese in a characteristically Sussex way – with a cricket match. After a solemn Mass in the cathedral there was a picnic lunch for about three or four thousand people, and then the Bishop of Arundel and Brighton's XI lined up against the Duke of Norfolk's XI on the famous cricket ground near the Castle. Miles's team was captained by the legendary Colin Cowdrey, and included David Frost, who was married to Miles's daughter Carina, as wicket-keeper. There was great applause when I walked out to open the batting with Michael Bowen, the previous bishop of the diocese. I would like to be able to say that we marked the occasion with a half-century opening stand, but Micky and I were both out within a couple of overs. But it was a great occasion, and with a strong innings from Crispian Hollis, the Bishop of Portsmouth, decent contributions from one or two other priests of the diocese, and some friendly manoeuvring, the Bishop of Arundel and Brighton's XI won – or was allowed to win.

8

Together yet apart

I awoke at 6 o'clock or so on 12 October 1984. When I switched on the radio I heard the news that a bomb had exploded in the Grand Hotel in Brighton in the early hours of the morning, and that a number of people had been killed or injured. Of course I knew that the Conservative Party annual conference was being held in the town, and I guessed that the Prime Minister, Margaret Thatcher, would have been staying at that hotel.

I thought straightaway, I should go. And then I instinctively picked up the phone and called Eric Kemp, the Bishop of Chichester. 'Look, Eric,' I said, 'have you heard about the bomb? I think the two of us ought to go down to Brighton together.' He said: 'Yes I agree.' Eric came over in his car, picked me up and the two of us drove down to Brighton. We found a place to park near the promenade and walked over to the hotel. It was scene of terrible chaos. The hotel's façade had a gaping hole, there were emergency services people everywhere, police were cordoning off various areas in case there was another blast, and there were people whose faces I recognized, cabinet ministers, wandering around, dazed and unshaven. It's strange, but at times like this, even people who have no religion seem to welcome the sight of a priest.

Eric and I went to the hotel where Margaret and Denis had been moved to from the Grand, and went in. We were in the lobby writing a note of condolence to send up to her, when we saw John Gummer, then the Conservative Party Chairman. He said: 'I think she would like to see you.' He rang up and the message came down: 'Would we go up?' So we went up and went into this little room. The Prime Minister was standing, wearing black, looking firm and composed, with Denis behind her and Robin Butler, the cabinet secretary, in the corner of the room. We spoke for a few minutes about the people who had been killed or injured; then she said: 'Bishops, will you pray with me?', which we gladly did.

My decision to pick up the phone to call Eric was spontaneous. It had become almost second nature to me to ask first, isn't this something we can do together? After we left Mrs Thatcher, Eric and I were able to speak to several other people in and around the hotel, including some of the injured and the bereaved. It was good for the two of us to be able to offer a little comfort to her and others during that terrible day. Somehow, when the leaders of different churches act or speak together, the effect is more than the sum of their separate parts. The instinct to only do on my own the things I couldn't do together with my opposite numbers in other churches had gradually developed over the years since I was a curate, and stayed with me when I came to Westminster.

Sometimes, when I look ahead along the ecumenical path, there seem to be so many trees lying across the road it's hard to see any realistic way forward. But then I look backwards, and in some ways the obstacles we have somehow managed to skirt round to get where we are today look even bigger. The decision of the Church of England to ordain women as bishops places another obstacle on the path to the unity. Humanly, it's difficult to imagine a time where there will be the mutual recognition of orders and the full communion between us that we pray for. But the road to Christian unity has no turning back. To live in harmony with the prayer of the Lord, 'that all be one so that the world believes' (John 17.21), means that we can never say, 'I will go this far and no further'.

As an eight-year-old I remember being proud of my mother when she willingly joined the Reading branch of the Sword of the Spirit movement. This was initiated in 1940 by Arthur Hinsley, the Cardinal Archbishop of Westminster, who together with George Bell, the Bishop of Chichester, wanted to bring all Christians together to work and pray for peace and a new world moral order. Ellen was more adventurous than my father. George took the more traditional view that risqué ecumenical experiments were likely to mislead the faithful and only raise hopes it would be impossible to fulfil. But in time of war one learned not only how to suffer together but also how to pray together.

When the much-loved Cardinal Hinsley died in 1943, the ecumenical momentum was somewhat lost. His successors as Archbishop of Westminster shared George's caution rather than Ellen's boldness. There were honourable exceptions, but in the years before the second Vatican Council and the publication in 1964 of its historic decree on ecumenism, the Catholic Church's commitment to Christian unity tended to fluctuate between the half-hearted and the openly hostile.

How well I remember my excitement and slight sense of alarm when, as a young curate, I read in the Council's decree *Unitatis redintegratio* (in English, 'the restoration of unity'): 'There can be no ecumenism worthy of the name without a change of heart, interior conversion, newness of attitudes and an unstinted love.' The unity of Christians, I was being told, was not just a prayer for the conversion of Protestants.

It demanded that I myself had to change. I was being challenged to alter my attitude towards fellow Christians, in a spirit of cooperation and love.

I had to overcome what I have come to realize are the three enemies of ecumenism: suspicion, inertia and impatience. To overcome suspicion I had to meet and become friends with fellow Christians. This was to turn out to become one of the great joys and blessings of my life. As I began to understand how much Christians hold together in our life of prayer and in our love of Jesus Christ, not only did my fears and wariness began to disappear, but I found myself enriched and enchanted by new friendships and new traditions of prayer and worship. I also had to combat inertia. I had to do more than merely assert that, 'Yes, of course I am an ecumenist'. I had to push myself to become active in ecumenical affairs, and foster joint Christian events in any way possible. And I also had to learn to let go of my natural impatience, and to realize that while the road to unity might seem interminable, the bumpy pilgrim path which all of us have to undertake is also one of hope, of cooperation, of love – and of surprises.

I suppose I began my personal ecumenical path in earnest during my years as secretary to Derek Worlock, between 1966 and 1970. Derek was as serious about ecumenism as he was about everything else, and we worked together to build ecumenical cooperation and friendship in the diocese of Portsmouth. When I left Derek to become a parish priest in Southampton, I was only there for a year before being sent back to Rome as Rector of the English College. But before I left there was one ecumenical occasion for which I will always be grateful. At a meeting of all the local ministers and clergy from the surrounding area, I found that I was the only one who lit up a cigarette. Never a heavy smoker, I was accustomed at that time to puffing on five or six cigarettes a day.

Looking round the table I remember saying to myself, 'Cormac. This will not do!' I gave up smoking from that day onwards. Ecumenism has some unintended benefits.

The six years I spent back at the English College were an opportunity to deepen my commitment to the ecumenical path and to develop new ecumenical contacts. I have already mentioned how much I learnt from Cardinal Jan Willebrands and gained from the deep spirituality and good humour of Norman Goodall, and I have described how we initiated an exchange between some of our students and ordinands from the Anglican theological college, Westcott House, Cambridge. This arrangement was my introduction to the Principal of Westcott, Mark Santer, whom I would encounter in another context some years later.

When I became Bishop of Arundel and Brighton in 1977 I was determined to do all I could to foster friendship and cooperation with other Christian leaders in Sussex and Surrey. The Bishop of Chichester, Eric Kemp, became a close friend, as did the Bishop of Guildford, Michael Adie, and his successor, John Gladwin. Eric was very High Church – much higher than me in fact. And there were lots of clergy in his diocese who were even 'higher up the candle' than Eric: one of his priests always used to ask his congregation to pray for 'Eric and Cormac' in the Eucharistic Prayer. I was amused and indeed pleased. When there was a big arms fair in Brighton in 1981, Eric and I joined the march to protest against the trade in weapons. In 1991, Michael Adie and I led a pilgrimage together to the ecumenical community of Taizé, a place of prayer and reconciliation. We hoped that our trip would serve as a living sign of our churches' commitment to each other.

I also formed lasting friendships with the leaders of the other Christian denominations. I remember on one occasion being asked to say a few words at the annual meeting of the Free Church Federal Council which was being held in Eastbourne. I began my short address extending warm greetings to them all. 'We Nonconformists must stick together!' I concluded, to loud and sustained applause.

Among the many memories I have of ecumenical initiatives during those years were the joint visits of Christian leaders to large conurbations in Sussex and Surrey. We would have a joint meeting with local ministers and clergy and then visit a prominent focal point in the town. The idea was to show that we were determined to act together whenever we could, and to encourage local Christian churches and communities to cooperate together and share in ecumenical events in their towns and neighbourhoods. I long to see Church leaders and their congregations and communities taking more risks, being more creative in making spaces where Christians can meet and pray together. When this happens, they find that they are already in the process of reconciliation because the one Spirit of God is already working in their hearts. Once we understand this, we are moved to a greater mutual love and a greater longing for unity, and we realize that we are travelling together as brothers and sisters on a road with no exit.

I used to say that the grace of ecumenism is in the local Church. There may be great events connected with the pope or the Archbishop of Canterbury, but when local Christians pray together, cooperate together, foster unity together, there the grace of the Holy Spirit is present and fruitful. During at least one Lenten period we encouraged the formation of joint Lenten groups, providing suitable material to help the participants to pray and work together. At the end of one such Lenten session we invited all the participants to meet together at Worth Abbey in Sussex for a service of thanksgiving and prayer. To our delight, nearly three thousand people turned up and the large Abbey church could scarcely contain everyone. It was a most moving celebration and the prayer and wonderful singing showed how much those Christians wanted to be together and grow in unity in faith and life.

What sort of other things might be tried? There might be agreements for a joint use of churches and other ecclesiastical buildings, agreements to share facilities for theological education and to have an exchange of students, and a joint exploration of new forms of worship and retreats in common. There could be more interchange of preachers at certain times, and more joint statements from church leaders on matters of national and urgent human issues. There are many opportunities here as well as challenges. What is needed are evangelical spaces within which Christians can grow together.

I spent some weeks in the Holy Land in 1984. It taught me that Christianity, in the world of the future, was going to have to live alongside people of no faith and people of other faiths, with a willingness to share what by the grace of God we have received, each in our own traditions. This new way for the Church means that we must learn to cherish diversity.

The diocese of Arundel and Brighton included Gatwick Airport, so it was my privilege to greet Pope John Paul II when he arrived in Britain on 28 May 1982. I remember climbing the steps of the plane with the papal nuncio and there he was, sitting in his seat, looking rather grim and determined. Perhaps he thought that because of the Falklands war there might be some protestors greeting him on landing. He need not have worried. The visit was a huge success, with over two million in all greeting him at the various venues and millions more seeing him on television. Pope John Paul had enormous stamina. I remember feeling quite weary after just three days. For me, the most moving moment in his visit was when he and the Archbishop of

Canterbury, Robert Runcie, jointly presided over a prayer service in Canterbury Cathedral. When I heard the pope say, 'Behold before us the past and the future! Behold before us the desires of so many hearts', tears came into my eyes.

There were amusing moments during those wonderful few days, too. When he was due to leave Scotland, the crowds sang 'Will ye no come back again?' The pope turned to Thomas Winning, the Archbishop of Glasgow, and asked him what the words of the song they kept repeating meant. Tom explained that the song referred to Bonnie Prince Charlie. 'Oh, I know him,' the pope replied, 'I met him in Canterbury last week!' Wrong Prince Charlie.

Very soon after the pope's visit I learnt that I would be the Catholic co-chairman of the Anglican-Roman Catholic International Commission (ARCIC). I think it was Richard Stewart, a lovely English priest working at the secretariat for unity in Rome, who put me up for the job. ARCIC had been established by the Archbishop of Canterbury, Michael Ramsey, and Pope Paul VI in 1967, and the first phase of work had been completed in 1981 with the publication of its Final Report. ARCIC's three 'agreed statements' on Eucharist, Ministry and Authority, followed later by painstaking 'elucidations' and 'clarifications', found fresh language to express treasure common to all of us. Although reaching agreement on Authority was to prove elusive, the statements on Eucharist and Ministry were generally well received and have been widely accepted. In many ways, it was an astonishing achievement, finding common ground on issues that had bitterly divided Christians since the Reformation. After the success of the pope's visit there was a a feeling that the work must continue.

We had our first meeting of ARCIC-II (the 'son of ARCIC' or 'Ben-ARCIC' as it soon became known in the trade) in Venice on 30

August 1983. The Anglican co-chair was the Bishop of Birmingham, Mark Santer, the former principal of Westcott. We were to become close friends. As Pope John Paul and Robert Runcie admitted in their common declaration establishing the new phase of ARCIC, 'We are well aware that this new commission's task will not be easy'. We were given a wider brief than to just carry on talking about doctrine. We were also asked to study the factors which prevent a mutual recognition of ministries, and to plan the stages along the way to reunion.

In the early years of my involvement in ARCIC, we had a real feeling of momentum. The spirit was with us. This has sometimes been described as the honeymoon period for ecumenism, and perhaps it was the high point of the movement towards unity, at least in terms of approaching full communion between the Churches. The great historian and theologian, Henry Chadwick, who with the Dominican priest-theologian Jean Tillard were the outstanding scholars among us, thought we could reach full communion in his lifetime. One of the early meetings was at Palazzola, the English College's summer retreat outside Rome, where a plaque in the refectory celebrates the students' first dinner after Arthur Hinsley's purchase of the villa in 1920, at which the guest of honour was Cardinal Gasquet, one of the main authors of the 1896 encyclical that declared Anglican orders to be 'absolutely null and utterly void'. I did not expect to see full doctrinal and ecclesial communion but I certainly thought we might get to the point of a mutual recognition of orders. That would have been a momentous step.

We would get together for our main gathering once a year at the end of the summer. We used to take it in turns to host the annual meetings. We went to Venice a few times, Paris, Vienna, and twice to Palazzola; we also had meetings in Durham, Windsor, Dublin, Edinburgh and Llandaff.

For me, the ARCIC meetings were a kind of annual seminar. They were hard work but very enjoyable: ten days or so of intelligent conversation with a small group of scholars and friends. There were twelve Anglicans and twelve Catholics, and the discussions were open and very frank. There were one or two members who I have to admit I didn't particularly look forward to hearing from, but everybody had to have their say. It was a joy and privilege to listen to Henry Chadwick and Jean Tillard unearthing from their profound knowledge of the Fathers of the Early Church new insights and reflections on the Church of today. They did a lot of the detailed drafting. Henry always seemed to be able to conjure up a phrase that would satisfy all of us, even when sometimes we might not be completely convinced that we really did believe quite the same thing. He always treasured a stole which the pope had given him.

The chemistry of the meetings was often surprising. The most heated disagreements were often not across the table, as it were, but between fellow Anglicans and fellow Catholics. The Catholics often found themselves more comfortable with the evangelicals than with the more high church or Catholic-minded Anglicans. They tended to share a more traditional approach to moral issues and to the interpretation of the scriptures. But personal friendships would cut across all these lines. At first, we would start with the Catholics celebrating Mass together and the Anglicans celebrating the Eucharist together, and then all of us coming together for Evening Prayer. But after the first year, I suggested we would attend their Eucharist one morning and they would attend our Mass the next day. I came to appreciate the Book of Common Prayer. I'd be very happy to swap Vespers for Evensong.

Henry said to me once: 'You know, Cormac, the reasons for our divisions are not fundamentally theological; it's just the sad fact that we've lived separately for 400 years, and we've developed different ways.' It was sometimes hard to get into the different mindset of our Anglican partners, but when we scraped away the froth of our tribal customs and jargon we kept discovering a common faith at a deeper level. Our first agreed statement, *Salvation and the Church*, brought us to a shared position on one of the most intractable issues to have divided Christians: the doctrine of justification. Then we went on to study the nature of the Church in *The Church as Communion*, before producing *Life in Christ: Morals, Communion and the Church*. This statement on morals proved a very difficult one for us to reach agreement on. Oliver O'Donovan, an Irish Protestant, did the heavy lifting, and I think the result holds up pretty well.

The most important document we worked on was *The Gift of Authority*. Of all the issues we discussed over the sixteen years that I was co-chair of ARCIC, authority was perhaps the most difficult. Agreement on authority – how the Church teaches, acts and reaches doctrinal decisions in faithfulness to the Gospel – is at the heart of ecumenical dialogue. Everyone seeking full visible unity between Anglicans and Catholics knows that this issue, more than any other, has become the most serious obstacle in our path. We had reached convergence on many subjects connected with authority in the Church, even an agreement on the primacy of the pope. But *The Gift of Authority*, which followed on two other statements from ARCIC-I, raised challenges for both Anglicans and Catholics. Anglicans were asked if they had any instruments of oversight or government which would allow decisions to be reached that would bind all the Churches of the Anglican Communion. And when major new questions arise which in faithfulness to Scripture and Tradition require a united response – where do Anglicans look for an answer? Anglicans hope with each succeeding Archbishop of Canterbury that he'll be the one who will lead them out of captivity, and heal its divisions over doctrinal questions. But I don't think anyone can. It seems to me that the way that authority is currently exercised in the Anglican communion leaves the Archbishop of Canterbury, whoever he is, in an impossible position.

Perhaps it's an irony that while some Catholics grumble that the Church is too bossy and heavy-handed in its exercise of authority, many Anglicans feel that their Church is becoming more fragmented precisely because of the leaking away of authority. If we raised some uncomfortable questions for the Anglican members of ARCIC, we had our difficulties on our side too. Does the way authority is exercised in the Catholic Church reflect the authority of Christ, who came 'not to be served but to serve'? Does magisterial authority in the Catholic Church always realize that those who exercise magisterium or teaching authority are themselves part of the *sensus fidelium*, part of the common mind of all the people of God? Perhaps the trickiest issue is the collegiality of the bishops. This is the teaching – reaffirmed by the second Vatican Council – that the bishops of the world share with the pope the responsibility for the governance and pastoral care of the Church. But by and large, the bishops have still not asserted their authority in the Church in the way that the Council envisaged. John Paul II and Benedict rather tended to leave the issue in the freezer. Francis, I think, is minded to breathe life back into it. Collegiality might prove to be the great battleground of his papacy.

On the first day of the meeting we had at Palazzola in September 1987, Pope John Paul paid us a visit, along with Cardinal Willebrands. Palazzola faces the pope's summer residence of Castel Gandolfo, on the opposite side of Lake Albano, so it was comparatively easy for him to drive over to meet us. We had lunch together in the refectory. There were five of us at my table, including John Paul, and the discussion was very lively. One of the members at our table spoke passionately about the difficulties of cooperation, not so much with Anglicans but between Christians and Muslims in the north of Nigeria, where he was from. We spoke about the discrimination faced by Christian communities in many parts of the world. I remember saying that, paradoxically, sometimes faith can be strengthened where there is persecution. The pope turned towards me and placed his hands firmly on the table. 'Yes, I agree; I agree.' To understand Pope John Paul you have always to bear in mind that his was a Catholicism that was forged in persecution and oppression. Only firmness and resolve had enabled it to survive.

In 1989 the Archbishop of Canterbury, Robert Runcie, paid an official visit to the pope in Rome. Mark Santer and I were invited to accompany him and we had a very eventful few days in Rome. I grew fond of Robert Runcie. He was kind, brave, and had a wry sense of humour. I remember being driven through Rome on our way to the Vatican escorted by five or six motorcycles with flashing lights, each mounted by a rider wearing a stylish uniform. Robert said to me: 'Ask the driver, how many motorcycles are in the pope's motorcade?' So I asked our driver in Italian: 'How many motorcycles does the pope get?' He replied laconically: 'Ten.' And of course Runcie had to ask: 'Why has the pope got ten and I've only got six?' The driver was silent for a while. Then he explained solemnly that there has to be *'una classificazione'* ('a classification'). Robert loved that.

Robert told me that he wanted to raise with the pope the question of the ordination of women, which was beginning to loom large in the Anglican Communion at that time. We had a formal meeting with the pope, Willebrands and Pierre Duprey of the unity secretariat, and Christopher Hill and one or two others on the other side. I thought

Robert would bring it up at this meeting, but he didn't. As we were going in to lunch afterwards, John Paul took Robert's arm and said, in very good English: 'Do not worry. You know, affective collegiality will lead us on to effective collegiality.' It was a lovely moment.

There were twelve or fourteen of us around the table and I was at one end. When you are having lunch with the pope you can't really start chatting with whoever is sitting next to you. There's only one conversation. So I started it off. 'Holy Father, I met a friend of yours this morning, or at least I saw him.' He asked me who it was. 'Dr Ian Paisley', I said. There was general amusement at this and we became more relaxed. Later on during the meal I took my chance to help Robert. 'Holy Father', I said, 'the Anglicans and Catholics on the Commission agree about very many things, but there are some things we disagree about.' The papal eyebrow was raised. 'Such as', I continued, 'the ordination of women.' There was a hush round the table. Robert took up the subject and laid the situation as he saw it before the pope. Others spoke. And then the room became still. Everyone waited to hear what John Paul would have to say. He turned to me and said: 'The ordination of women – and what is ARCIC going to do about it?' End of conversation.

The issue of the ordination of women became an increasingly awkward issue for us. The Catholic Church asserts that in faithfulness to Scripture and the constant Tradition of the Church, it does not consider itself authorized to admit women to priestly ordination. Both Paul VI and John Paul II reiterated this teaching. In 1992, the Church of England authorized the ordination of women and the first women were ordained in 1994. With the decision of the Church of England to ordain women, the honeymoon was certainly over. It was a terrible moment for me. My hopes were crushed. Notwithstanding the doctrinal agreements on the Eucharist and Ministry, the identity and validity of the priest exercising ministry was now a crucial factor, because the person who is ordained is linked to the nature of the sacrament of Holy Orders. The differences between us on the ordination of women touched on the agreements that had been reached regarding ministry and authority in the Church.

The ARCIC process continues. There's now an ARCIC-III in place, the grandson of ARCIC perhaps. It met for the first time in Bose, Italy, in 2011, with the Archbishop of Birmingham, Bernard Longley, as the Catholic co-chair. There is no going back or reneging on the promises that were made to continue seeking fuller communion between all Christians. The future of the Church cannot be anything other than the continuance of the ecumenical endeavour. It has not proved possible to achieve full Eucharistic communion between our two churches, but the very real communion that exists between us is something that we should build on and cherish. Recent years have shown that there are many matters in which Anglicans and Catholics, together with other fellow Christians, can and should work together, not only in serving others and challenging an increasingly unbelieving and secular world, but also in faithfulness to what the Lord Jesus Christ said in his last prayer: 'May they all be one, Lord, may they be one as you are in me and I in you, so that the world may believe' (John 17).

Basil Hume wasn't terribly keen when I told him that I would be going to Rome with Robert in 1989. 'Why are you going?' he asked. I explained that the pope was meeting the Archbishop of Canterbury as the head of the Anglican Communion, not as the head of the Church of England, and as co-chair of ARCIC it was natural that I would be expected to be there. Basil was ecumenical, but only up to a point. I think there was a little bit of Basil that considered himself the real head

of the Church in England. When he visited Anglican monasteries and
cathedrals, he would be thinking, 'Shouldn't this be ours?' His heart
wasn't entirely in it really.

John Wilkins, the editor of *The Tablet*, interviewed Basil for his
70th birthday, and his piece appeared on 27 February 1993. My copy
of *The Tablet* would usually arrive on a Thursday, and, like every
bishop, I would always pick it up with a mixture of anticipation and
a certain mild trepidation. I went straight to the interview, in which
Basil looked back on his life with his usual candour, especially his time
at Westminster. Then, towards the end, I came across a sentence that
made my jaw drop. Wilkins had asked Basil about the significance of
the recent decision by the Church of England to admit women to the
priesthood. 'This could be a big moment of grace', he was reported to
have replied. 'It could be the conversion of England for which we have
prayed all these years.'

I could hardly believe he'd been quoted accurately. I rang him
immediately and asked him: 'Basil, did you really say that?' Basil
replied: 'Yes I said it; what do you mean?' There was something of my
father's traditional Catholic approach to ecumenism in Basil. George
didn't think Catholics were any better than Protestants. But he thought
that Catholics had the truth, and that Protestants were in the wrong.
So he prayed for the conversion of Protestants, as I did when I was a
boy and later when I was a seminarian in Rome. That changed at the
Council. We didn't stop believing that the fullness of faith was found in
the Catholic Church, but we no longer claimed that we had a monopoly
on truth. The conversion that we prayed for now was a conversion of
heart that would start with ourselves. We certainly no longer wanted to
be seen to be seizing on difficulties in the Church of England as opportunities for making converts. I persuaded Basil to issue an explanation

of what he had said, a copy of which he sent personally to George Carey, and to some extent the hurt was assuaged.

There were some in Rome who thought that the ordination of women would lead to serious divisions in the Church of England, and a large influx of former Anglican clergy being received into the Catholic Church. Basil was slightly misled by Graham Leonard, the Anglican Bishop of London, whom he'd been meeting regularly. He thought that as many as a third of the Anglican clergy might seek to join the Church. When Basil asked Pope John Paul what he should do, he was told, 'Be generous, be generous'. I was amazed at the eagerness of Rome to accommodate Anglican priests wishing to join the Catholic Church. Their ordinations were fast-tracked – Graham Leonard was ordained within a few weeks; and, most significantly, the ordination to the Catholic priesthood of married Anglicans was waived through. I wasn't against this, but I was keenly aware that we would have a sensitive task to explain to our clergy that while married Anglican clergy could be ordained as Catholic priests, celibacy was still mandatory for them. In the end, several hundred former Anglican clergy were ordained as Roman Catholic priests, usually after a preparatory period of about two years.

I came to like and admire Rowan Williams, who succeeded George Carey as Archbishop of Canterbury in December 2002, very much. He has that Welsh gift of being able to see two, if not three, sides of every question, and to be able to defend each of them with dazzling conviction and eloquence. In December 2006, Rowan and I, together with other Church leaders, went on a pilgrimage to the Holy Land for four days. It was a poignant experience. We went as an act of solidarity with the Christians of the Middle East, to express our desire for peace in this land of conflict, and to draw attention to the plight of the members of these brave and ancient churches. The first Christian believers were from these towns and villages. Now, their continued existence there hangs by a thread. I felt their desperate fear and isolation. The thought that I might live to see the departure of the last native Christian believers from the region fills me with sorrow and shame.

A poignant moment occurred when we visited a hospital and orphanage run by a French order of religious sisters. Many unmarried mothers, both Muslim and Christian women, had found sanctuary there after being rejected by their families. To our surprise, on our arrival two sisters placed babies in our arms. These were children who had been abandoned by their mothers and rescued by the sisters. The sisters told us that there were two precious gifts that they were able to give the children: a name, and their love. Holding those children in our arms in Bethlehem made it a Christmas I will never forget.

9

'The elephant is out of the bottle'

Pope John Paul II was beginning to look very frail, but he still had a word for each of the new archbishops as they approached him one by one to receive the *pallium*. As he placed the narrow woollen scarf over my shoulders, he took my hands in his and leaned towards me.

'Westminster', he said. And then, after a pause, he added solemnly: 'Important. Important.'

I didn't need reminding of the scale of the responsibility I had been asked to take on. I'd learnt of my appointment a few months earlier. It was 10.30 p.m. on Saturday, 2 February 2000. I was just about to get ready to go to bed when the telephone rang. It was our press officer, asking with some irritation why I had not told him that I had been appointed the Archbishop of Westminster.

I didn't know what he was talking about.

'It's the headline on the front page of tomorrow's *Sunday Times*.'

I went to bed, puzzled, and of course the next day the telephone never stopped ringing. People were calling me to ask me if it was true, probing me, teasing me, congratulating me. It was very awkward. Everyone naturally thought I'd had a call from the papal nuncio to tell me I was the pope's choice to be the next Archbishop of Westminster and that I had leaked the news. But in fact I was still in the dark. And I still don't know where the leak had come from.

Finally, on Sunday night, I got a phone call from the nuncio, a Spaniard, Pablo Puente, asking me if I could drive up to see him the next morning.

The nuncio's official residence is a detached villa in Wimbledon. I drove through the gate and up the gravel drive to the front door. As Archbishop Puente opened the door to let me in, he smiled broadly and said: 'Well, Father, the elephant is out of the bottle.'

The archbishop's grasp of English idiom made up in colour what it lacked in precision.

So the newspaper story was true. How they got hold of it, I never found out. I learnt later that the journalist Christopher Morgan had been saved from a great disaster because he had been convinced the Archbishop of Liverpool, Patrick Kelly, was about to be appointed, and he'd cleared the front page for that. Then he'd called John Wilkins to check he'd got his story straight. It wasn't the only time I had the impression that the editor of *The Tablet* had better contacts in Rome than any of the bishops did.

I drove back up from Storrington to London on the following Monday in the evening to stay the night in Archbishop's House on Ambrosden Avenue, behind the cathedral, before the press conference the following morning, at which my appointment would be confirmed formally. At the same time, it was announced that Vincent Nichols would be the next Archbishop of Birmingham. Cormac to Westminster, Vincent to Birmingham: 'the dream ticket', one of the papers dubbed it.

Jim Curry, Basil Hume's former private secretary, met me when I

On a visit to Sri Lanka.

With the Director of the Muslim College, Zaki Badawi.

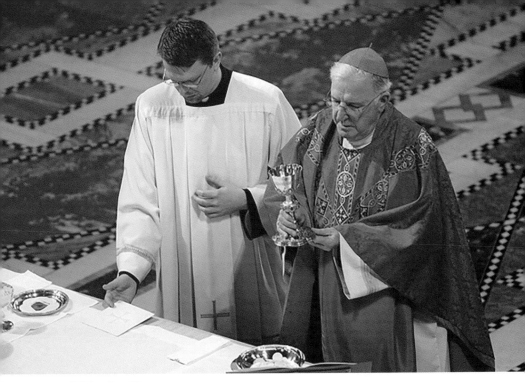

Celebrating Mass.

At a press conference with Archbishop (now Cardinal) Vincent Nichols.

A joyful meeting with Archbishop Desmond Tutu.

Preaching in the open air, Lourdes.

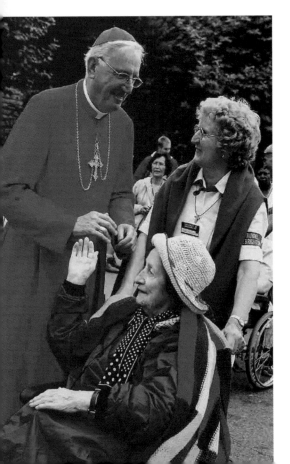

With pilgrims at Lourdes.

Attending the Church of England General Synod, 2009.

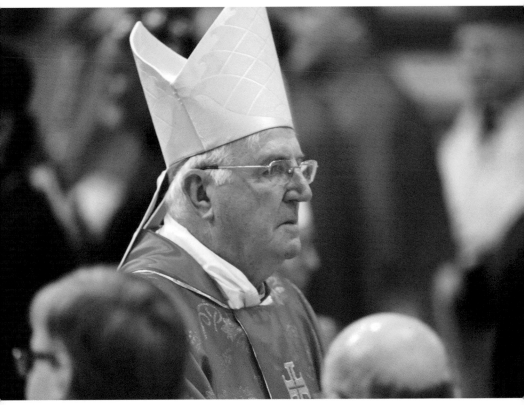

In procession at the Mass for the election of a Roman Pontiff, 2013.

With Pope Francis, 2013.

With Her Majesty the Queen and the Duke of Edinburgh.

arrived, and I remember we went into the living room of the cathedral clergy house next door, where Victor Guazzelli, the retired auxiliary bishop, was living. Victor was sitting with his back to us, watching the television. Jim quietly crept up to him and tapped him on the shoulder. 'Victor, turn round, and you'll see your new archbishop.'

Victor sat still for a few moments, and then he wheeled round in his chair to look at me. There was a long pause while he looked me up and down. 'Thank God', he said. I'm not sure who he'd thought he'd see, but he had obviously been half-expecting that his new bishop could have been someone worse.

Of course, after Basil told me when he was dying that I might have to follow him, I knew it was a possibility. Basil couldn't be sure what the pope would decide after his death, but I realized that it might come about. The prospect didn't cause me sleepless nights. I prayed about it, of course. And I asked one or two people I trusted whether, if I were to be offered it, I should accept, given my age and my experience. I was 67 that summer, but my health was pretty good.

Jim Curry told me later that when all the expert pundits had been bandying names around the kitchen table in Archbishop's House my name had been in the frame, along with David Konstant, Pat Kelly and Vincent Nichols, but no one had me down as the favourite.

There were one or two blots on my copybook. I'd spoken in support of the ordination of married men. I'd had a ticking-off about the letter I wrote to *The Tablet* about *Humanae Vitae*. And of course I was known as the co-chair of ARCIC, and I'm not sure everyone in the Vatican was entirely on board with the ARCIC process. But I was known a bit in Rome. I had been rector of the English College, and three other rectors – Wiseman, Hinsley and Godfrey – had gone on to be made cardinals. So perhaps that was a plus.

I was surprised. When I learnt that I had been appointed as Bishop for Arundel and Brighton, I felt I would be able to cope with the responsibilities that came with it. But I never expected I'd go on to be Archbishop of Westminster. But the good Lord has his own plans and that is how it came to be.

When I got the news, I told my sister Catherine, and then my brother Brian, who was retired. They were both delighted. And my eldest brother Jim and his wife Anne were thrilled to bits. Surprised, too. They all thought that after twenty-three years as bishop in Arundel and Brighton the moment had passed when Cormac might have another job in him.

The religious sisters who had lived in Archbishop's House and taken care of Basil's everyday needs had to leave and this meant I had to find another group of sisters who might replace them. I knew from my own experience the vital difference it made to live beside a community of sisters who prayed and worked together and welcomed visitors, not just to the wellbeing of the bishop but to the spirits of everyone associated with the household. Unfortunately, the Franciscan sisters who had been with me in Storrington were unable to come with me to Westminster. I approached Sister Mary Thomas, the Superior of a convent of sisters in Burgess Hill, and asked her if she could possibly spare three of the sisters and she kindly – and bravely – agreed. Archbishop's House is a large and rather gloomy building but Sisters Clement, Barbara and Pius made it a warm and welcoming home.

Twice a day I joined the three sisters and my priest-secretary in the private chapel, for Mass and morning prayer and then for evening prayer. In turbulent times I clung to the soothing rhythm and regular pattern of prayer all the more tightly. It is an extraordinary gift, which has enriched my life. I single out Sister Clement, who has always been a wonderful help and friend to me. Sister Damian, who acted as my loyal secretary when I was in Arundel, also agreed to join me in London for a few days each week. The dedication of these kind and patient women and, indeed, of so many others, goes often unsung. I am glad to sing it here.

I was installed as Archbishop on Wednesday 22 March. The Cathedral was packed with priests, religious and people from all the parishes of the diocese, and there were also the representatives of the royal family and of the cabinet. George Carey, the Archbishop of Canterbury, gave a very nice little speech of welcome. As I've mentioned before, there were a few smiles when I began my sermon with the story of the stone I had come across when I was out walking on one of the Scottish islands. On it was written, *Pilgrim Cormac*, and, underneath, the words, *He went beyond what was deemed possible.* I suppose there were some who were a little surprised at how far I'd come; few can have expected to see a 67-year-old asked to lead the largest diocese in the country.

Instructions had been given that nobody was to be admitted into the cathedral without a ticket, as every seat had been reserved and there were concerns about overcrowding. I was surprised a few days later to meet a resourceful Irishwoman who told me she had managed to get in without a ticket.

'How did you manage that?' I asked her.

'Well,' she said, 'I went to the ushers and asked if I could I come in even though I had no ticket. They refused. I kept asking and they kept on refusing. So then I told them I'd come all the way from Ireland. They relented when they heard this and let me in. Of course,' she added, 'I didn't tell them I had come all the way from Ireland forty years ago!'

I can't remember expounding any particular plan for the diocese in my sermon that day, but I already had a fair idea of the task that lay in store for me. I soon settled on what my priorities would be, too.

I knew that the first thing I wanted to do was to meet the two auxiliary bishops, Jim O'Brien and Pat O'Donoghue, and the other leading priests as well as the parish priests and all the priests of the diocese. I quickly realized that life as Archbishop of Westminster was utterly different to my experience as Bishop of Arundel and Brighton. It wasn't only that I had a very much larger diocese, with many more parishes and priests. The Archbishop of Westminster is normally elected as President of the Bishops' Conference, so suddenly I found myself responsible for the relationship between the bishops of England and Wales and the Holy See. Since it was going to take a few years before I could get round the diocese to visit the parishes one by one, I invited all the clergy of the diocese to come to Archbishop's House in groups for simple sandwich lunches, so I could meet and greet them all and say a few words to each of them individually.

It was a start. I looked forward to getting to know each of them much better in the succeeding years. I also invited all the women and men religious of the diocese to come to the cathedral and to a reception. Again, it was a frustration not to be able to spend more time with each community, but I was able at least to greet them and to be able to say a few words of encouragement to them all.

We are probably all inclined to go on too long. I certainly had a sense that I was running out of steam towards the end at Arundel and Brighton, and I think Basil had been treading water a little bit over the last few years. So there was a general feeling in the diocese, especially among the priests, that perhaps it was time for a change. The diocese had been carved up into four areas, each with its own auxiliary bishop and its own little curia, making decisions about evangelization and parish outreach and so on. It felt to me almost as if the diocese had become four mini-dioceses. I made up my mind pretty quickly to try to unify the diocese again. I knew that there might be some opposition. Catholic priests, on the whole, tend to like things to stay pretty much as they are.

I also felt the diocese needed a pastoral plan that would involve the diocese as a whole. Spiritual renewal has to start from the bottom up, with 'the domestic church': small groups of people meeting together to pray and to read the scriptures in light of their everyday experience. I was still inspired, just as I had been as a young priest in Portsmouth, by the old Yves Congar idea that it is in small communities that the gospel can come alive in people's lives. I was determined to initiate a spiritual renewal process that would unite the whole diocese, but I knew it would take imagination and hard work and perhaps a bit of cajoling to get the priests on board.

So I had a fairly clear idea of what I wanted to do. And I knew I didn't have long. Eight or nine years, I reckoned, so I thought, if I'm going to do anything I have to do it fairly quickly. I knew I would need a good, loyal team around me. I inherited Jim Curry from Basil; he had a good working knowledge of the diocese. Jim stayed on for a year and half as my private secretary, and saw me through. I started to line up a couple of new auxiliary bishops, Arthur Roche and George Stack, who would be confirmed in office early the following year.

There were a few awkward corners to negotiate. There was a popular and charismatic priest who had been in his parish far too long. I moved him on, but then I appointed someone in his place who wasn't able to cope. A mistake. Within a month or two a group from the parish came to see me. Not to tell the archbishop what he should do, of course – they were too savvy for that – but they made their feelings clear. It was one of the few times that, having made an appointment to a parish, I changed my mind. But I realized that he wouldn't have lasted six months.

Those first few weeks were a time of … well, excitement is the wrong word, but I found myself thinking that I was in the right place. I knew I would need help, of course, but I was starting to crystallize in my mind what I wanted to do. And I found that I was beginning to enjoy myself. I'm not sure where it came from, this feeling, not of over-confidence or complacency, but a sense that, even if it wouldn't be easy or straight-forward, I would be able to cope with whatever was thrown at me. I'd been a bishop a long time, and although of course Westminster was a very different sort of operation to Arundel and Brighton, I felt I'd seen most things and would be able to adapt reasonably well to the new role. I think the feeling also came from the way my mother would always encourage me. She always made me feel that it was all right to have ideas, to try things.

In late June, Vincent Nichols and I set off for Rome to receive what is called the *pallium*, a kind of stole or scarf of wool which is placed over the shoulders of all new archbishops by the pope on the feast of Sts Peter and Paul as a sign of their particular jurisdiction, usually a large metropolitan diocese such as Westminster or Birmingham. I returned from Rome at the beginning of July. I was feeling ready and eager to get back to work.

10

Shame and anguish

This is the most difficult chapter I have to write.

The issue of child abuse by some priests and its consequences for the Church have caused me more pain and anguish than any other issue in my long episcopal life. But I know that this was nothing compared to the pain, damage and anguish suffered by the victims of abuse.

A few weeks after Pope John Paul had placed the *pallium* over my shoulders on the morning of Wednesday 19 July 2000, there was a special report on the BBC *Today* programme that revealed that in the 1980s, while I was bishop of Arundel and Brighton, I had allowed a priest whom I knew to be a paedophile, Michael Hill, to continue serving as a priest in the diocese.

The abuse crisis had already inflicted terrible damage to the credibility of the Catholic Church. The perception was – and who could question it? – that decisions had been made to move priests who were paedophiles, rather than to report them to the proper authorities. Church leaders had put the reputation of the Church first, rather than the suffering and needs of victims and survivors. When some victims and survivors had had the courage to come forward, they had not been listened to, or, worse, believed.

When I went downstairs to the public affairs office on the morning of 19 July, the whole place was in turmoil. Everyone had heard the report on the radio. Michael Hill had been convicted and imprisoned for sexual offences in 1997 and jailed for five years, but details of the civil claims that some of his victims had brought against the Church were only revealed to the BBC after my appointment to Westminster. I knew that this story would create by far the greatest media frenzy to have hit the Church in the UK.

My secretary and my little team of advisors looked at me with a mixture of alarm and dismay. The phone was ringing off the hook. The BBC called to ask me to appear on the radio that lunchtime to answer the allegations made in their report.

'Are you going to resign?' I was asked. It was a question I was to be often asked over the next eighteen months. I wasn't able to dismiss the BBC's story. In the early 1980s, when I was Bishop of Arundel and Brighton, I had received a complaint about Michael Hill and his behaviour with a minor. After sending him away for counselling and then receiving another complaint, I removed him from his parish and sent him to a therapeutic centre in Stroud which was then run by a religious order. He did not complete the course and remained for some time in secular employment.

One day he came to see me. He cried with remorse and begged on his knees to be given some work as a priest. I remember, after he left, going back through the files. I'd received reports on Michael Hill from different psychiatrists and counsellors, and the assessments were inconsistent. One recommended that although he should not be put back into parochial ministry, he could perhaps be given a job where no children were involved. The post of chaplain at Gatwick Airport was vacant and I decided that he should go there, as I believed there would be no prolonged contact with children on their own in that work.

Of course, I was very wrong. I should have reported him to the police and the social services. I didn't. I will always look back on my decision with sorrow and shame.

There were many victims of Michael Hill's abusive behaviour. He was convicted in 1997 and jailed for five years, and after confessing to further offences was convicted and jailed again in 2002. It was said that I moved Michael Hill from parish to parish, knowing that he was a paedophile. That was not true. I was gravely mistaken in allowing him to return to limited ministry as chaplain at Gatwick Airport, but I had moved Hill from his parish in Merstham to Godalming because he had completed a normal stint and was due for a move, and I moved him from Godalming because there had been a complete breakdown of his relationship with his curate and they couldn't live in the same house.

For the next two years it felt as if I was always going on the *Today* programme and being harangued by John Humphrys, or appearing on *Newsnight* being grilled by Jeremy Paxman. I started to dread reading the newspapers because every now and again there would be a reference to the Hill affair.

For eighteen months or so the media storm raged on. It was hard not to feel that we were being 'got at'. But I knew it wasn't right just to blame the media, as many in the Church and some around me were suggesting. In some of the interviews and at some of the press conferences I did feel a tangible hostility. But I knew instinctively that the real problem wasn't with newspaper reporters or broadcasters. The problem was in the Church and we had to address it. The Church must be a place of safety for children, if it is to be anything.

This was later echoed by Pope Benedict. When he was asked if he thought the Church had been unfairly singled out for criticism over the abuse scandal, he replied: 'No. We deserve this humiliation. How did we manage to remove ourselves so far from the truth?'

To my shame, it only gradually began to sink in just how much damage abuse causes to victims – pain and damage which will be part of their lives for ever. I met victims of clerical abuse many times, privately in London and then later in Ireland, as an apostolic visitor, at a series of public hearings and private meetings. I recognized and felt their fury and deep anguish and distress. Two cases in particular profoundly affected me. A woman who had come along with a friend told me her story. She was now in her forties. She had been abused by a priest as a young child, in a terrible way. And a priest who had himself been abused when he was a boy by his parish priest.

Perhaps the thing I was told most often was that the Church had been arrogant and had failed to listen. It is hard to listen, to really listen, to really hear the anger and the shame and the loss in people's lives. Unless we listen and include the very people who have suffered the most, we will get things wrong. There are many victims of abuse in the Catholic Church in England and Wales and across the world. To each and every one I extend my heartfelt sorrow and apologies for what they have endured.

The great lesson for all of us – certainly the most important lesson I had to learn – was that, first and foremost, we have to listen to victims, to put those who have been abused by priests at the centre of the story.

It isn't good enough just to compare ourselves with other institutions, to make the rather self-serving point that the abuse of children is increasingly being uncovered wherever adults are in positions of power and authority over children. The Catholic Church should be, above all, a place where children, and all vulnerable or fragile people, are completely safe and cared for. If we cannot be a place of security and tenderness for the sick and the poor, the Church has lost its way.

Coming so soon after the joy and quiet satisfaction of receiving the *pallium* in Rome – not a reward or a prize, but a sort of token of the hopefulness and sense of purpose I had begun to feel as I prepared for this final leg of my journey as a priest – it came as a shattering blow. Each morning when I joined the sisters and my secretary for morning Mass and then came downstairs to join the team of advisors in my office, I felt as if I had let everyone down.

A week or two after the story of Michael Hill broke, I was approached by Lord Nolan. 'Is there anything I can do to help?' he asked.

I knew Michael Nolan slightly; he had a grandson at a special school in my old diocese. He had been asked by the John Major government to chair the enquiry into standards in public life which had soon become known as the Nolan Committee on parliamentary sleaze. He had recently retired as a law lord.

I thought over his offer and rang him back. 'Yes, Michael,' I said, 'I think there is.'

I knew instinctively that we had to have not just an investigation into what happened in the case of Michael Hill, but a root and branch review of child protection in the Church. It would have to be completely independent and – if it was to have any credibility – it would have to have a strong, experienced leader of complete integrity. And we needed to act quickly.

Lord Nolan agreed to chair an independent committee. Its aim would be to stop, insofar as it is humanly possible, any further case of child abuse by clergy. I asked him, 'Michael, what do you need from me?' And he said, 'Help me get a good group together.'

He was a master of the trade. He knew exactly what he wanted, right from the off. First, he asked to have another judge to work beside him, Sir Swinton Thomas, the retired Lord Justice of Appeal; and then he said he had to have a secretary to take minutes at the meetings and hearings and to draft the report. He had someone in mind, a former civil servant: Chris Brearley.

Nolan insisted that throughout the review the interests of the child – not of the Church, or even of the parents – would be paramount. The nine-person committee was in place by the middle of September. The other members were David Veness, the assistant commissioner of the Metropolitan Police; Caroline Abrahams, director of public policy for NCH Action for Children; Hilary Eldridge, director of the Lucy Faithfull Foundation which works with abusers; Dr Maurice Lipsedge, a psychiatrist; and Gill Mackenzie, a senior probation officer. There were also two priests on the committee, Bishop Peter Smith and Mgr Jack Kennedy, the child protection co-ordinator in the archdiocese of Liverpool. A tenth member, the Revd Tim Bryan, detective chief inspector, Metropolitan Police, joined the committee in October. Apart from the two judges and the two priests, the other six on the committee were not Catholics, and some of them were a little sceptical at first. Perhaps they thought it might be some sort of whitewash.

Nolan was to conduct the review immaculately. Regular meetings, two hours long, with just the right people in the room. Sometimes these commissions can last for a couple of years; the Nolan Committee had its report and recommendations completed within six months. Michael was ready to come and speak to the bishops at their May meeting the following year.

I couldn't be sure what would happen. I hadn't really consulted the other bishops about the Nolan Committee, I'd just gone ahead and set it up. When we were setting up Nolan there was nobody else doing anything similar that we could compare it with, a model that we might follow. Nolan made over eighty recommendations, including the immediate reporting of a disclosure to the statutory authorities, much tighter vetting of students for the priesthood, the laicization of offending clergy and the establishment of a national database so that paedophiles could not find refuge in other dioceses. Professional child protection co-ordinators would be employed.

The bishops agreed unanimously to adopt Nolan's recommendations. It was extraordinary really – in the Catholic Church each bishop is responsible for his own diocese, on the basis that local problems require local solutions. Getting joint statements or common protocols and procedures agreed by all the bishops in a single country has often proved difficult. And Nolan's recommendations were not going to be cheap to implement. When it came to dealing with the abuse of children by priests there has been a temptation for bishops in some parts of the Church to say, 'There's no problem in my diocese', or, 'I'll sort out the problem in my own way.' The bishops of England and Wales all recognized that the Church had to get to the roots of the issue of sexual abuse by priests, even if it would require dramatic and decisive action. We all endorsed Nolan's top priority: that the Catholic Church in England and Wales should become an example of good practice in the prevention of child abuse, and in responding to it. Michael Nolan died in 2008. I will be forever grateful to him for his generous help and assistance to me and to the Catholic Church in England and Wales at a time of great need.

Five years after the publication of the Nolan Report, another independent committee, chaired by Baroness Julia Cumberlege, examined the protection procedures in every diocese in England and Wales and made further recommendations in the light of the experience of the previous five years. An independent commission to oversee strategy and policy making was set up, and a separate professional service was created to support and train those in the Church involved in safeguarding.

Some priests had felt that the bishops had swung in a panic from being blind to the interests of victims to being blind to the rights of accused priests. I worried about the morale of the clergy. Priests were feeling that they were all now seen as potential abusers. One had said to me: 'Nolan is all very well, but once anyone makes an allegation to you about me, I'm finished'. One of the recommendations of the Cumberlege review was that, if an allegation of abuse had been scrutinized by social services and the police and it had been decided that no action should be taken, then the diocese might make its own enquiry, and while it could still decide that the priest should continue to be suspended from work in the diocese, if it was believed that there were no grounds to the allegations the priest would be able to return to his parish.

In retrospect, I should have done more to encourage the heads of the religious orders and the abbots of the monasteries to sign up to Nolan's guidelines more quickly. I regret not inviting them to join the bishops when we were discussing his recommendations, some of the problems that we have seen in recent years in monastic schools would have been averted.

I think it can honestly be said that whatever the mistakes and mishandling of allegations of child abuse in previous years, the Church in England and Wales now has stringent measures in place for the safeguarding of children and vulnerable adults. There is still much work to do. But we have made a start.

At the height of the crisis, I had discussed resigning with one or two friends and close advisors, but no one thought it would make the situation any better. The attention and the anger were to a considerable extent focused on me; I was seen as the leader of the Church in England and Wales. If I were to resign, the anger would not go away, it would just be transferred onto someone else. I knew something had been very wrong and I knew it was my job to start to put things right.

I'd been foolish and naïve and, perhaps, I had drifted into that little space where kindness blurs into weakness. It's an old failing. Rather than tackle a difficult issue, I can be inclined to leave it aside and to turn to something more cheerful and positive. As rector at the English College, there were times when I should have been tougher, and then as a bishop over the years, there have been one or two occasions when I ducked a really difficult decision. Perhaps I lack the ruthlessness that really successful leaders have.

The daily routine went on, and became increasingly precious to me. Morning Mass, prayer, and so on. I remembered my mother's voice saying to me when I had got my thumb trapped in a door, or was in some sort of pickle, 'Cormac, these things are sent to try us'. I've always been someone who accepts whatever comes. Sometimes, we fall back on the old saying, 'We all have crosses to bear'. There was a little bit of that.

Why did bishops and religious superiors so grievously mishandle allegations of child abuse? It wasn't – at least in my experience – that we were driven by a determination to keep scandal about the Church out of the newspapers at all costs. I'm sure there was an element in my thinking of wanting to protect the reputation of the Church. But a more convincing reason, I think, lay in the way in which episcopal authority was exercised. Like every bishop, I was told at my ordination that I should have a special care for my priests, to treat them as brothers and be merciful in dealing with their faults. In cases of abuse, however, how wrong we were not to think first of all of those who had been abused.

At the forefront of my mind when I became a bishop was the care of the priests of the diocese. I wanted any priest who was in a hole to be able to feel they could come to me to talk about it. The Church had, in a way, become my family, and the priests had become brothers. However, when allegations are made about a priest we now know strict procedures must be implemented. We now understand more about the addictive nature of paedophilia. Paedophiles act under compulsion, and are likely to reoffend. I now know the terrible damage done to the victims of abuse, the consequences of which remain with them for the rest of their lives. The new guidelines are necessary, precisely because this protective instinct is so strong. Otherwise a bishop could be led into making the mistake I did over Michael Hill, and allow the instinct to forgive to override caution and good sense.

I was slow to grasp the impact of abuse. Perhaps like a lot of people from relatively happy and secure family backgrounds, I have such a strong positive image of the family that I found it difficult to face up to the fact that families can be places of terrible abuse and violence, as well as of love and security. In some ways, the abuse crisis forced me to re-examine everything I had come to understand about the Church as 'the family of the Church'.

Of course, we have to look again at the way that we train and prepare men for the priesthood. When I was a student in Rome in the 1950s, it wasn't that we were shielded from the darker aspects of sexual desire. In morals we were taught about incest as if it were not totally uncommon. But we were never taught about the abuse of children. There was genuine ignorance about paedophilia. And there is much more attention paid now to human and pastoral formation, as well as the spiritual and intellectual. In my time, most of the seminarians had come to the college straight from school and junior seminary at the age of 18 or 19. We said our prayers and we passed our exams. We are conscious now that in the selection and formation of a priest there should be the nurturing of a mature, well-balanced person. As well as the bishop and his team, serious assessments are always given by a psychiatrist and other experienced lay people in the selection of a candidate for the priesthood.

Pope Benedict has been heavily criticized for his failure to get to grips with the problem of the abuse of children by priests. This is unfair. The real blame lies with the leadership in the local churches. When the problem came to the surface in my time at Westminster, I didn't see how Rome could help and it didn't occur to me to ask. It was clear to me from the start that it was our problem and it was my responsibility to address it. And when the Nolan Report was published, I think we may have sent a copy to Rome. But I didn't think about Rome really. We just got on with it.

In the years since Nolan and Cumberlege, many bishops of other countries have told me that they wish they had similar guidelines in place. I wrote to Pope Benedict to suggest that he write to the presidents of the bishops' conferences throughout the Church asking them to establish a Nolan-type review. That, I think, would have been the right way for Rome to be involved – not taking responsibility for clearing up the mess themselves, but insisting that the local churches address the problem. The bishops' conferences would have been welcome to use the Nolan and Cumberlege recommendations as a sort of template which could be adapted to their local needs. When I next met Benedict, he thanked me for my letter, and said, 'I'll do it.'

In 2012 during Pope Benedict's visit to the UK, after I retired, I was part of the papal party and was driven around London in the same car as Benedict's secretary of state, Cardinal Tarcisio Bertone. He had never been to England before and I enjoyed pointing out the sights. When I asked him, 'Whatever happened to my letter?', I never got a clear answer.

I was moved and humbled when I read of Pope Francis's meeting with victims of abuse in July 2014. They stayed with him, attended his Mass and met with him individually. In his homily at Mass Francis spoke of the experience of survivors of abuse – for some suicide, for some addiction to drugs or alcohol, for others difficulty in making or sustaining relationships and a distancing from the Church they may once have loved. He asked them for their forgiveness and then he added that if, when they had had the courage to come forward and tell a bishop or a priest about their abuse, they were not listened to or believed, he even more profoundly asked for their forgiveness. It is good that Pope Francis has now taken further practical steps to try and ensure that the safeguarding of children and vulnerable adults is a top priority in every country, in every diocese, in every parish in the Catholic Church worldwide.

11

Into the deep

During the difficult summer of 2000 I went to the papal nuncio, Pablo Puente, and said: 'Perhaps Rome should put off making me a cardinal until all this dies down.' But my concerns were dismissed. On 21 February 2001 I was created a cardinal by Pope John Paul II. It was one of his last consistories and there were forty-four of us from all over the world collecting a scarlet biretta and skullcap, including the Archbishop of Buenos Aires, one Jorge Bergoglio. It was the first time I was to meet the future Pope Francis.

It was a happy time for me as most of my family and friends were in Rome for the occasion and their enjoyment and pleasure and pride were mine too. To become a cardinal is a great honour and privilege which carries with it the responsibility not only to help, support and advise the pope, but also to be one of those who would elect his successor.

I also received a scroll from the pope with the name of my titular church. In the early days of the Church the parish priests in Rome used to elect the bishop, and therefore it had become been the custom for cardinals to be made a titular parish priest of a church in Rome. To my delight and astonishment, my titular church was to be one of the most beautiful in the city, Santa Maria sopra Minerva, next door to the

Pantheon, run by the Dominican fathers. The basilica was built over the ruins of the temple of the Roman goddess of wisdom, Minerva, in the eighth century. The only medieval gothic church in Rome, it houses the bodies of Italy's patron, St Catherine of Siena, and the patron of artists, Fra Angelico. It also has a Christ bearing the Cross by Michelangelo.

I am not the first Englishman to be the titular of the church. I share the honour with the Dominican cardinal, Thomas Philip Howard of Norfolk and Arundel, great-grandson of the English martyr, St Philip Howard. I often visit there. It is, as it were, my parish church in Rome.

Though the Nolan Committee was now holding its meetings and was due to report in a few weeks' time, I knew there was still a long road ahead before the problem of child abuse in the Church would be resolved. It was always going to be my most important priority. But I was determined to turn my attention to the needs of the diocese. What I'd learnt from the way the bishops had all signed up to Nolan's recommendations was that even though my reputation might have been dented, I could still offer leadership. In fact, I'd found that in some ways, my public fall from grace made people more willing to be helpful and supportive.

When Heenan came to Westminster he tried to do what he had done in Leeds and Liverpool: visit all the parishes, make all the decisions. That's impossible in a large diocese like Westminster. I met the priests in groups, and said a Mass in a different parish every Sunday, but I knew I would have to delegate. I wasn't a Derek Worlock – absorbed in every detail. I had a good idea of what I wanted to do as archbishop, but I needed a good leadership team to work with me.

The first new auxiliary bishops to be appointed were Arthur Roche, a Yorkshireman who went on to serve as Bishop of Leeds and was then called to Rome to serve as secretary to the Congregation for Divine Worship and raised to the rank of archbishop, and George Stack, who had been the vicar general in the archdiocese and who was later to be appointed Archbishop of Cardiff. We were joined by Alan Hopes, who had been a priest in the Church of England for twenty-six years before his reception into the Catholic Church, now Bishop of East Anglia, and Bernard Longley, an accomplished musician, now Archbishop of Birmingham. Finally, in 2006 I was glad when John Arnold was appointed auxiliary, and he continued to be an invaluable aid and collaborator with Vincent Nichols after my retirement, before being appointed Bishop of Salford in 2014. My auxiliary bishops were an enormous help to me and I could count each of them as friends.

I was lucky, too, in the three priest-secretaries I had during my nine years of office: I inherited Jim Curry from Basil; then Mark O'Toole, now Bishop of Plymouth, whom I have mentioned before; and finally Martin Hayes, now vicar general. They were loyal, discreet and patient of their boss's ways, a wonderful help to me in my trials and troubles, joys and achievements.

We use to meet every Friday to discuss the running of the diocese. Whatever shortcomings I might have as a leader, I've always been pretty good at chairing a meeting, at getting different sorts of people working well together. It's enjoyable and satisfying to guide people as they take up new responsibilities, and to see them flourish in new roles.

Whoever was the vicar general would be doing 'the moves', shuffling priests around the parishes. This was Alan Hopes's job for a number of years. The temptation is to do the smaller parishes first, as these switches were usually easier to arrange. It's best, though, to tackle the larger, prestigious parishes, or the parishes where there might be problems, first. When I'd been in Arundel and Brighton, I used to move parish priests every eight or nine years or so, and on the whole that's what we did in Westminster.

Arthur Roche had been the punctilious general secretary of the bishops' conference when I arrived: a key job in the Church, heading the various offices and departments in Eccleston Square that support the bishops in their work. When he became an auxiliary, I found an equally assiduous replacement in Andrew Summersgill; like Arthur, he was a Leeds priest. Andrew was a good-natured and efficient link between me and the other bishops, and helped me in particular in my role as vice-president of the Council of European Bishops.

I consulted the priests before I dismantled the area system. The change wasn't universally welcomed. The majority of priests were happy with the division of the diocese into four mini-dioceses, each with its own auxiliary and a self-contained administration. Each of the areas was the size and had the same number of Catholics as one of the smaller dioceses, so I could see the rationale behind it. But I wanted to create a sense of unity in the diocese. Once I felt that had been established, after a couple of years we went back to what we called a 'light touch' area system, with the auxiliaries having a special link to particular areas and clusters of parishes.

As well as a more unified diocese, I longed for a spiritual renewal programme that would reach out to everyone, families and single people, older people and young people, all those groups who sometimes get ignored, and to which all the priests could contribute, so they would be involved in something wider than just their parish.

My experience as a priest and as a bishop over the years has been that spiritual renewal starts from below, in the experience of sharing our faith with others in families and small groups. Although some people find it easy to fit into a parish community, a smaller group allows everyone to have a voice. When a dozen or so meet together, there is more fellowship and intimacy, and trust and confidence are more likely to develop, so that people who might feel intimidated or lost in a larger gathering are encouraged and inspired to talk and go further and deeper on their faith journey.

What has often struck me is that the influence of Christians is most tangibly felt in our culture not by pastoral letters or press releases from Archbishop's House or television appearances by church leaders, but by the actual witness of the people of God in their ordinary everyday lives. This is a core lesson that has remained with me over the years, and my belief in small communities became one of the first building blocks of our renewal project.

I knew that my vision of small communities might not be an easy sell to the priests of the Westminster diocese. For some of them, it seemed a quaint import from Arundel and Brighton. Small groups of parishioners gathering in each others' homes to read the Bible and talk about their faith might work in a leafy Surrey suburb or a seaside parish in West Sussex, but it was unrealistic to expect it to take off in Poplar or Dollis Hill.

In our little planning team, we often quoted a Latin phrase beloved of John Paul II: *Duc in altum* … ('Put out into the deep … and lower your nets for a catch'). These were Jesus' words to Peter, who had worked hard all night and caught nothing, and it remains a compelling vision for the whole Church. Peter's trusting reply, 'At your word, Lord', became the name we gave the programme. I knew we were taking a risk. Perhaps the doubters would prove to be right, and in spite of all hard work our nets would remain empty.

I had several meetings with priests where I explained my plans for renewal. I invited them to respond. There was muted enthusiasm. Of course it was easier in a way in Arundel and Brighton. I had been dealing with about 130, 150 priests. Now I was dealing, if you count the religious, with more than 400. The religious run nearly forty parishes in Westminster – that's the size of a small diocese. I had to get them on board as well.

I decided to get all the priests of the diocese together for three days to discuss the renewal programme. We needed a place large enough to accommodate several hundred priests and religious for three days. There was no church facility large enough. When the venue was finally announced, there were some raised eyebrows. Butlins holiday camp in Bognor Regis? Are you serious?

Although it was a cold November day in 2002 when we arrived, the fairground was open, the rides and the carousels were in action, and the famous Redcoats were there, all smiles, to show us to our chalets. There was a slightly surreal feel to it. I had persuaded Cardinal Danneels to come over from Belgium to speak to us, and we asked a well-known theologian, John McDade, to be our 'theologian in residence'. They were both effective. We also had an American speaker, a bit over the top. There were murmurings from some of the priests that they were being steam-rollered.

Eventually, the priests came on board. Perhaps it was the Butlins' breakfasts that did it. Whatever doubts and reservations were felt at the end of the day's meetings, every morning we all came down to a fantastic cooked breakfast of eggs and bacon and everyone's spirits lifted.

Was the spiritual renewal programme a success? It's always possible to see the glass as half full or half empty. Over 20,000 people participated in the 2,000 or so faith-sharing groups which were set up in parishes throughout the diocese. After three years, we had a congress to celebrate its achievements in the cathedral. Its indefatigable director, Canon Stuart Wilson, caught the mood when he said, 'We have a new vision in the diocese and in our parishes and a new understanding of being part of a vibrant community', and John McDade said, 'Perhaps what we're seeing with the success of "At Your Word, Lord" is the Church being made from below'.

The launch of 'At Your Word, Lord' was marked by a colourful and vibrant ceremony at Wembley in September 2003. As over 10,000 people marched into the great arena to celebrate the Mass that would begin our journey of renewal, I looked around and felt, in spite of our problems and failures, a sense of togetherness, a feeling that the 'family of the Church' could become a reality.

I always took a break for a few days every year after the Easter celebrations. On Thursday 31 March 2005 I returned to London when I heard that Pope John Paul had taken a turn for the worse and was not expected to live.

The abiding image of his papacy may well be the final one: of St Peter's Square filling with young people standing in serene silence, many of them holding candles. The Lord was coming to take his servant to the reward prepared for him; and it was enough to be close to that fading life on Friday night to feel the nearness of God to us all.

I waited at Archbishop's House on the Saturday all day long and in the early evening the news came through that the pope was dead. Immediately I went out to the piazza in front of Westminster Cathedral and said a few words to the media. I put my thoughts together for a homily for the funeral Mass held in Westminster Cathedral the following day, and on the Monday there was a service of remembrance in the cathedral attended by a huge number of civic and ecclesiastical dignitaries, including Prince Charles and Camilla Parker-Bowles and the Prime Minister, Tony Blair with his wife Cherie.

As I reminded the mourners in the cathedral, it had been an epic papacy. Pope John Paul was, unquestionably, one of the great Christian figures of our time. When he was elected in 1978, Karol Wojtyla believed that the Holy Spirit was summoning not only one particular individual to the papacy, but the Polish Church, and its experience of clinging tenaciously to the Gospel in the face of official atheism and totalitarian oppression. We realized just how significant that witness became when he returned to his homeland for the first time as pope, triggering a fever for freedom that would soon sweep across iron curtains and armed borders. And he was just as tenacious in his challenge to a Western world locked in its own forms of oppression: the idolatry of the marketplace, the quicksand of relativism, the subjection of human life to the god of individual self-fulfilment. For all that people have tried to place him in categories of right and left, radical and conservative, Pope John Paul II confounded them time and time again. He was too big for those categories.

These were a momentous few days, but for a priest there's a sense in which every death is the same, when a familiar routine clicks into action. There are prayers to be said, services to be prepared and arrangements to be made. The right words have to be found for a grieving family. A priest lives with dying every day. It's what he's for.

Early the following morning I flew to Rome for the funeral of Pope John Paul II and the election of his successor.

12

'Habemus papam'

I know Rome pretty well. It can occasionally be a place of agitation and heightened emotion. But nothing prepared me for the extraordinary ferment that seemed to have seized the city when I arrived late on Monday night, 4 April 2005, two days after the death of Pope John Paul II.

Four million people were gradually descending on Rome from all over the Catholic world, many of them young, often with nowhere to sleep. They had come to queue patiently, often for more than twenty-four hours, to file past the body of the late pope, laid out inside St Peter's Basilica, to pay their respects and to pray for the repose of his soul. Six thousand journalists and broadcasters were due to arrive to cover the funeral, and television crews were taking up sometimes precarious positions on roofs and terraces overlooking the square.

It was an atmosphere of quiet reflection and noisy speculation, of grief and pride and thankfulness, and of fear and hope for the future of the Church. The babble of reporters and Vaticanologists mixed with the solemnity of the great ceremonies and the moving sight of millions of people remembering a great pope who was also a Christian soul in need of their prayers. I had never experienced anything quite like it before.

For seventeen days the Catholic Church would be without Peter and in a deep spiritual sense it was incomplete. It is no wonder that the cardinals, who have the duty to elect a new pope, are urged to go as quickly as they can to Rome on the death of a pope and to prepare for the election of a successor. I had packed hurriedly. I knew I was going to be in Rome for at least a fortnight, and perhaps longer. No one knows for sure how long a conclave will take. I travel fairly light. I have a Breviary at the English College, and I always keep a spare set of cardinal's robes there.

On Tuesday morning I went straight into a meeting with the other cardinals. In between popes, technically at least, the cardinals are in charge of running the Church. The 'general congregations', as they're called, met each day that week in the synod hall, a modern lecture theatre with microphones and good translation facilities, once in the morning and then again in the afternoon. Our meetings were less interesting than you might think. Discussion was dominated by detailed preparations for the pope's funeral, which was due to be held on the Friday. There was very little talk about the election of his successor.

Our meetings were presided over by the dean of the College of Cardinals, Cardinal Joseph Ratzinger, who sat at a long desk facing us. Apart from the US Cardinal William Wakefield Baum, he was the only one among us who had been at the funerals of Popes Paul VI and John Paul I and at the elections of the successors in 1978, nearly twenty-seven years previously. Cardinal Ratzinger was a deft and efficient chair. He was not necessarily the cardinal that we each knew best, but he was the one cardinal that almost all of us knew well, and who knew each of us. As the cardinal prefect of the Congregation for the Doctrine of the Faith for twenty-four years, we had all visited him at the Palazzo del Sant'Uffizio. On the many occasions that I had been to call, first as Bishop of Arundel and Brighton and then later when I moved to Westminster, he was unfailingly courteous, intelligent and, above all, kind. I would always have a little list of issues and concerns in my pocket when I called to see him. He would greet me with a shy smile and then bring out his own little list, and then we would each go through our items in turn. I enjoyed my meetings with him, even when I left with a little less than I'd hoped for. Our conversations were always open and honest; I always felt I could share whatever was on my mind, and I always felt I had been genuinely listened to.

I found it impossible to walk across St Peter's Square on my way to our meetings without being beseiged by reporters wielding microphones. The vast majority of the journalists were Europeans or Americans. Cardinals from Japan or Nairobi or wherever were being hounded by journalists from Chicago or Arkansas, demanding to know who they would be voting for in the forthcoming election. So at one of our first meetings, I proposed to the cardinals that we continue to give interviews to the press, if we wanted to, but only up to the funeral of Pope John Paul on the Friday, and not in the nine days afterwards, between the funeral and the conclave to elect the pope's successor. This would give the cardinals who were experienced and relaxed media performers a few days to say their piece to camera, but would also allow for a period of prayer and reflection away from the media frenzy for all of us. Cardinal Ratzinger looked relieved. 'I think that the suggestion of Cardinal Murphy-O'Connor is a good one', he said. And that was enough.

For three days the body of Pope John Paul was laid in state, first of all in the papal residence, after which his body was placed in St Peter's Basilica. He had hoped to be buried in his native Poland but he left the final decision to the cardinals, and we decided it would be more appropriate for him to be buried where so many of his predecessors had been laid to rest, inside St Peter's. The line of mourners to see the body stretched for miles, but the Swiss guards allowed cardinals to jump the queue and on several occasions I was able to take one or two people in with me. Sr Damian and Sr Clement from the house were among those who took advantage, and I was pleased to be able to welcome Rowan Williams and conduct him through a side entrance into St Peter's. We prayed together before the body of the pope.

Rowan returned a few days later for the funeral. He was the first Archbishop of Canterbury to attend a pope's funeral since the Reformation. Ecumenical Patriarch Bartholomew was also there – the first Ecumenical Patriarch to attend a papal funeral since the Great Schism. There were innumerable kings and queens, presidents and prime ministers there too, of course. It was said to have been the single largest gathering in history of heads of state and it was estimated that over four million people were present in Rome for the occasion, and that it had the greatest-ever audience for a televised event. I was touched and delighted that Prince Charles attended, representing the Queen – he put back the date of his wedding to Camilla Parker-Bowles to be there. I have always admired the Italian police and social services but never more so than during these few days, when they had to cope with the many thousands of people roaming the streets during the day and spending the nights in sleeping bags and makeshift shelters in the piazzas.

Cardinal Ratzinger presided at the ceremony with great dignity. We were all very moved as he spoke in his homily of his friend's life as bishop, cardinal and pope, and emphasized his devotion to Mary and to the Divine Mercy of Christ. Then he came to those extraordinary final few days:

None of us can ever forget how on that last Easter Sunday of his life, the Holy Father, marked by suffering, came once more to the window of the apostolic palace and one last time gave his blessing, '*Urbi et Orbi*'. We can be sure that our beloved pope is standing today at the window of the Father's house, that he sees us and blesses us. Yes, bless us, Holy Father. We entrust your dear soul to the Mother of God, your mother, who guided you each day and who will guide you now to the Eternal Glory of her Son, Our Lord Jesus Christ.

I was deeply moved. I will never forget seeing the bearers of the coffin turning to present the body of Pope John Paul to the vast crowd one last time, and hearing the applause and feeling the tears and the memories come flooding back. Together with the other cardinals, I followed the coffin from the piazza back inside St Peter's, and accompanied him to his final place of rest.

The funeral was followed by nine official days of mourning, the *novemdiales*, marked by a Requiem Mass each day in St Peter's. The cardinals had the weekend off, and then we resumed our daily meetings in the synod hall. The conclave would start the following Monday, 18 April. Again, our discussions that week were less exciting than you might imagine. Much of our time was spent in going line by line through the manual of instructions and the formalities that had to be observed during the election of a pope. We spent very little time discussing the needs of the Church or the qualities required for John Paul's successor. Several of the cardinals aged over 80, who would not be joining us in conclave, took the opportunity to bend the ears of the younger men at great length.

There were 183 cardinals in all, but those aged over 80 had been ineligible to take part in a conclave since Pope Paul VI had reformed the rules for the election of a pope in 1971. Paul had also intended there to be no more than 120 cardinal electors at any one time; when John Paul died there were 117 of us under the age of 80. John Paul had, in fact, appointed another cardinal '*in pectore*' ('in his heart') in 2003, but his identity was never made public and John Paul took the secret with him to the grave. Two of the cardinals eligible to vote, including Jaime Sin, Cardinal Archbishop of Manila, who had been at the 1978 conclaves that had elected Pope John Paul I and then John Paul II less than two months later, were too ill to travel, so that left 115 cardinal-electors. There were 11 cardinals from Africa, 10 from Asia, 58 from Europe (including 20 from Italy), 2 from Oceania, 22 from North America (including 11 from the United States) and 12 from South America.

Of course, there were private meetings in the evenings all over Rome. I was able to meet and get to know some of the other cardinals better, and to hear them talking about the situation of the Church in different parts of the world in a more informal way. I hosted a private supper at the English College with a handful of cardinals – we brought them up the back stairs – and I went to a meeting hosted by Cardinal Achille Silvestrini, who although unable to take part in the conclave because of his age was nevertheless an influential figure. Other cardinals were engaged in similar get-togethers during the week.

The retired Archbishop of Milan, Carlo Maria Martini, was present at one of the conversations I took part in. He embodied, for me, the spirit of the second Vatican Council, which has always inspired my life as a priest. He was someone of outstanding intellect, and a lovely man. I admired him enormously and was very fond of him. I had first got to know Martini when I was rector of the English College in the 1970s and he was a professor of biblical studies at the Gregorian. He was five years older than I was, and knew my cousin Jerome, another New Testament scholar, well. I remember a time when we were both at the same conference in Ireland and we went for a long walk. We were both fairly new in our dioceses. I'd been ordained bishop for the relatively small diocese of Arundel and Brighton, while Martini had been plucked by Pope John Paul II straight from academia to lead the archdiocese of Milan, one of the most prestigious and high-profile positions in the universal Church. He was generous with his time and open about the difficulties he was facing. We agreed about the importance for a bishop, whatever the size of his diocese, of having a pastoral plan. 'And how's your plan going in Milan?' I asked him. 'Well,' he said, 'it's going quite well, but there is a problem. There are others in the diocese who also have a plan. And it's a very different one to mine.'

I think all during the time of Pope John Paul there was a tug in a slightly different direction, or at least a wish for the tone of voice to be a little different. The differences were not over doctrine but over emphases and priorities. Among some of the European cardinals in particular, there was a hankering for a more pastoral style, a longing for a shift of the focus of attention from the centre of the Church to the peripheries. Some even among the cardinals felt that the reforms of the Church initiated at the second Vatican Council had been smothered to some extent. There were always tensions between this group and some in the Vatican. My own feelings were ambivalent. I had welcomed with excitement the spirit of renewal and reform in the Church set in train by the Council. There was no doubt that the momentum of reform in the Church had been slowed down. But I also remember from my conversations with Cardinal Heenan all those years ago, and other priests and lay people since, how many had felt that the ground was shifting under their feet, as if the changes initiated by the Council – welcome though they were – had unleashed an unexpected storm.

Pope John Paul II had been needed to steady the ship. Perhaps a leader would be needed now with different emphases and priorities; or maybe the right time for a change of tack would come later.

If there had been a conclave a decade earlier Martini might, I think, have been elected pope. Now he was old and unwell and there was no obvious candidate to carry forward what you might call the reforming agenda. The thoughts of the cardinals were still dominated by the death of John Paul II. The overwhelming mood during those days was of 'safety first'. Where could we turn for a steady hand on the tiller?

In the synod hall, we continued our scrupulous preparations for the conclave and we continued to hear speeches from several non-voting cardinals who wanted their voices to be heard. At one of our last meetings we had ballots to decide who would be the scrutineers at the election; we even had a ballot to allocate each of us the number of our room at the Casa Santa Marta, where we would all be staying during the conclave.

I arrived there with my bags on the Sunday evening before the conclave was due to start. Although I usually stay at the English College, I'd stayed at the Casa Santa Marta a few times before, and it was comfortable enough. It was plainly furnished but I had a good bedroom, a little study and a bathroom. It was the first time the residence, built on the orders of John Paul II a few years previously, had been used for a conclave. Previously the cardinals had suffered in cramped quarters inside the Apostolic Palace, in unheated makeshift accommodation with distant bathrooms. I unpacked my bag. They had removed the telephones from the rooms and there were shutters on the windows. I'd brought my mobile phone, but I knew there was no point trying to use it. The signals were jammed.

The next morning, Monday 18 April, we concelebrated the Mass

Pro Eligendo Romano Pontifice (for the election of the Roman pontiff) in St Peter's before returning to the residence for lunch and a rest. At 4.30 in the afternoon we assembled in the Hall of Blessings and processed to the Sistine Chapel, singing as we went along the Litany of the Saints. When we arrived in the Sistine Chapel and went to our seats, we sang *Veni Creator Spiritus* ('Come, Creator Spirit'), a hymn asking the Holy Spirit to come into our hearts at this solemn moment. Vatican carpenters had been hard at work since the funeral, installing a wooden false floor over the pavement to even out the different levels. There were two rows of long tables and chairs along the opposite walls of the chapel, and a table at the end, in front of the altar, where the three cardinals who had been chosen by lot to act as scrutineers would sit.

Each of us in turn took an oath promising that we would not reveal any of the results of the voting, not only then but also after the election. We sang the Te Deum, a hymn of praise to the saints, asking for their intercession in the momentous choice we were going to make. Then the master of papal liturgical celebrations, Archbishop Piero Marini, gave the order '*Extra omnes*' ('Everyone out'), the members of the choir and the Swiss guards and others left, and the doors of the Sistine Chapel were closed with a great thump. Marini waited while Tomáš Špidlík, a non-elector cardinal, gave the meditation, then they left, and we were alone. I looked round at the other 114 cardinals. 'One of us', I remember thinking, 'is going to leave here wearing a different cassock.'

We had our first ballot that evening. On the table in front of me was a list of names of all the cardinals and several rectangular pieces of paper, with the words '*Eligo in Summum Pontificem*' ('I elect as Supreme Pontiff') printed on the top and a space below for me to write the name of my preferred candidate. We each wrote a name on one of the ballot papers, folded it in half, walked in turn to the front of the chapel, held up the ballot in the air, placed it in a saucer and then tipped it into a silver urn shaped like a flying saucer.

Before we lodged our ballot paper in the urn, we each said: 'I call as my witness Christ the Lord, who will be my judge, that my vote is given to the one who before God I think should be elected.' When it was my turn to vote I remember looking up at this point at the great painting on the wall behind the altar: Michelangelo's 'The Last Judgement'. I walked thoughtfully back to my seat. It was a journey I had to make only four times before we had our successor to Peter.

After we had all voted, one of the scrutineers shook the urn. As each ballot was pulled out, it was marked by the first scrutineer, passed to the next for examination, and then read out by the third. Each ballot was pierced with a needle and thread and strung together. I kept score on my list of cardinals by putting a tick next to the name receiving a vote as they were read out.

It was a very solemn occasion, but after we had all voted there was a bit of chit-chat between the cardinals while the scrutineers counted the papers. I was sitting next to Ed Egan of New York. The little group around me included Lubomyr Husar of Lviv in the Ukraine – one of the three Eastern Catholic cardinals to participate in the conclave, an extraordinary man – Severino Poletto of Turin, José da Cruz Policarpo of Lisbon and Jorge Bergoglio of Buenos Aires, Argentina. We'd all been created cardinal by Pope John Paul at the same consistory in February 2001, and we generally used to sit close together at meetings of cardinals. I called our little group 'La Squadra' ('The Team').

After the ballot on the Monday evening, we all went back to the Casa Santa Marta for supper together in the refectory. After the plates had been cleared away, we sat around in little groups talking. Smoking was prohibited in the residence, and Cardinal Policarpo had to sneak outside for his after-dinner cigar.

The next morning, we were up early for Mass and breakfast, and then there was a call to tell us that the shuttle buses had arrived to collect us and drop us at the Sistine Chapel. I preferred to walk through the Vatican gardens with one or two other cardinals. It takes five or ten minutes, around the back of the basilica. I noticed one or two Swiss guards skulking in the trees of the Vatican gardens and wondered if they were checking that we weren't making discreet phone calls. Already, I had a feeling that the conclave would be over before the end of the day.

There were two further ballots in the morning, one after the other: there was no break between them. Even on this momentous occasion, there was still something of the schoolboy from Reading in me. I wanted to see for myself the famous stove that was used for burning the ballot papers. It was in the corner by the main entrance to the chapel. There was a little funnel above the stove that went up through the roof, and there is some special mixture that they add to the used ballot papers that makes the black smoke, and another mixture that makes the white smoke. This time, it was the mixture for black smoke that was used.

After the ballots had been counted and burnt, we went back to the Casa Santa Marta. We had a typical Roman lunch: pasta, a main course and fruit. Wine was on the table. We ate quietly. There was a sense of serenity among us. After three ballots, a consensus was emerging, and many cardinals switched their votes at this point. We returned to the Sistine Chapel for the fourth ballot with a sense that a different mixture might be needed to be added to the papers when they came to be burnt in the stove.

As the votes were counted, it became clear before very long that one name was getting more votes than anybody else. He had to get

77, two-thirds plus one, to be elected, as it was essential that the pope would have the support of the great majority of cardinals. How well I remember as the voting for one cardinal reached the 70s. The atmosphere in the Sistine Chapel was very tense, as we all wondered if he would reach the required number. The hush was only interrupted by the sound of the scrutineer calling out the name of the cardinal who had received a vote. When the name 'Joseph Ratzinger' was called out for the 77th time, we burst into applause.

The voting continued until all 115 votes had been registered. Then Cardinal Sodano, the secretary of state and vice-dean of the College of Cardinals, approached Cardinal Ratzinger, who was sitting at the edge of a line of cardinals, with his head bowed.

'Your Eminence, do you accept to be the Supreme Pontiff of the Catholic Church?' he said.

Cardinal Ratzinger looked up. We held our breath. He could have said, 'No, I cannot'. There was a pause before he answered, 'I accept as the will of God'.

Cardinal Sodano then asked: 'What name do you wish to be called?'

This time, the answer was immediate. 'Benedict'.

And now, suddenly, he was no longer 'Cardinal Joseph Ratzinger'. There is no ceremony; no anointing; no blessing. From the moment he accepts and he is named, he is Pope Benedict XVI. In the relief and excitement of the moment we all turned to each other, smiling, shrugging, embracing. We watched the mixture being added to the used ballot papers that would produce white smoke, indicating to the thousands of people gathered outside in St Peter's Square – and to those all over the world watching on television – that a pope had been elected.

I suspect every cardinal enters a conclave with a name up his sleeve – just in case. I've sometimes been asked what name I would have chosen in the most unlikely event that the electors had turned in desperation to me. I had toyed with Adrian, the name chosen by the only Englishman to have been elected pope, and Gregory, who had sent St Augustine to England. And once I woke up in the middle of the night and I thought, what about Cormac the First!

In a room just outside the chapel a Vatican tailor had been waiting with three white cassocks: one large, one medium and one small. Pope Benedict went out and reappeared after about ten minutes wearing one of the white cassocks. He sat down and we all went up to him one by one. I kissed his ring and declared my loyalty to him and my fidelity to the Faith that he was to serve in a very special way. He spoke to us for a few minutes, asked for our prayers and then said: 'Now we must go out to the balcony and give the blessing to the people.'

So we all went out together and I stood in the window next to the middle window, through which Benedict would appear. It was a strange feeling to hear the cardinal deacon, Jorge Medina Estévez, declare, *Annuntio vobis gaudium magnum. Habemus papam* ('I announce to you a great joy, we have a pope'), not over the radio or television, as I had for previous papal elections, but standing a few feet away.

After he had blessed the crowds, Pope Benedict asked all the cardinals to join him for supper later that evening at the Casa Santa Marta. I had time to collect my stuff from my room before Pope Benedict arrived. When he came in, now in his white cassock, we all clapped him. We had a pleasant meal together, after which Cardinal Sodano got up and said: 'We must now drink the health of our new pope.' So we raised our glasses, and then Sodano said: 'Will nobody sing?'

There was a pause. This is where I made my big mistake. I started to sing something I was sure everyone would know well, *Ad multos annos vivat*' ('May he live for many years …'). Just the ticket, I thought. But nobody joined in. I had a quarter of a second to decide whether I would continue or not. Well, I did sing the rest of it and then we sang another song. So ended perhaps the most unforgettable day of my life.

On the final day of Pope Benedict's visit to Britain in 2010, after he had addressed the bishops at St Mary's College, Oscott, I was able to propose a toast to him as he was leaving. I apologized for disturbing the proceedings on the evening of his election but said that I was sure that my fellow bishops and I would sing the '*Ad multos*' now with great familiarity and fervour – which we did. It was a fitting end to what had been an extraordinarily successful visit.

Joseph Ratzinger was very brave to accept the papacy. No one is obliged to do so. I remember an occasion when Rowan Williams was in Rome and was invited to lunch with the pope, and I accompanied him. It was a very relaxed and enjoyable occasion. But it was when I asked Pope Benedict how the book he was working on, *Jesus of Nazareth*, was progressing that he became really animated. It was very hard, he told me sadly, to find enough time for the study necessary to complete the book amid the many duties of his office. It occurred to me that he had accepted the papacy as the will of God and not out of choice. He had longed to retire and devote himself to prayer and study.

All the cardinals make a solemn promise to keep the details of the voting at the conclave secret, including, of course, how they themselves had voted. Although I've had a few kickings from the press, I've always felt that whether you like it or not, speaking to journalists and to broadcasters is part of the job, and I've always liked and got on with most of them on a personal level. The press are always going to get up your nose from time to time; they wouldn't be doing their job properly if they didn't. As my years in Westminster went on, the support I was getting in my media work improved. Austen Ivereigh was a very astute press aide; then I had the benefit of Alexander DesForges' tact and experience; now I am fortunate to have the help and expert advice and counsel of Maggie Doherty. But I was still capable of the occasional *faux pas*. In an interview after the conclave I let slip that 'they' had elected Pope Benedict, which was interpreted as an admission that I hadn't voted for him. This was not necessarily a correct reading of what had happened.

Many of the cardinals had become increasingly irritated by inter-ference from curial officials in the affairs of their dioceses, and several were uneasy about the Vatican's failure to address the damaging scandal of sex abuse. Although I was close to many of the cardinals who hoped for a new papacy with a more pastoral tone, determined to reform the curia and prepared to loosen the reins of control from the centre, I became more and more aware as I listened to the cardinals in conclave that the overriding feeling was that the Church needed continuity, at least for a few years. Whoever followed John Paul II would inevitably be in his shadow. Everything he would do would be immediately compared with a great predecessor. Any attempt to change tack would meet with fierce resistance, and lead to division. I came to the view that the time was not yet ripe for a decisive change.

It is said that God writes straight with crooked lines. In the years that followed, the frustrations which had been felt by some of the cardinals at the conclave of 2005 became more widespread. Various financial shenanigans and public relations disasters; the shameful way that the abusive behaviour of Marcial Maciel, the founder of a wealthy order of priests, the Legionaries of Christ, had been ignored; the Vatileaks scandal: all added to a mounting sense of disarray and dysfunction inside the Vatican. Perhaps its 'poverty' or helplessness had to be laid bare before the Church was ready to turn to a radical reformer. Benedict, a highly intelligent and sensitive man, had to bear all this. I think the years of his papacy will be seen as the time when the Church went through great suffering and shame but that this was a necessary part of the mysterious rhythm of death and resurrection which belongs to its history. It is that history, yet to be written, which will perhaps see the events of Benedict's papacy in a different light.

Sometimes, short pontificates can act as essential gateways: they can release possibilities, set the stage for a vital next act. Both John XXIII and Benedict XVI were important transitional figures. John opened the way between the Church exemplified by Pius XII and the Church of the second Vatican Council and the reforming papacy of Paul VI. And we needed Benedict to allow us to draw breath after the monumental papacy of John Paul II, a grand performance that left the audience gasping and needing a little while to settle down before it would be ready for the appearance of another virtuoso.

13

A voice in the public square

This is a memoir, a sketch, rather than a detailed account of my life. But these four contrasting cameos will give you a flavour of the kind of issues I had to deal with and the decisions I had to take in my nine years as Archbishop of Westminster. There was the question of the admission of Catholic bishops to the House of Lords, inherited from my predecessor, Basil Hume; the dramatic and painful case of the conjoined twins that arose in my first year; the Iraq war and the correct response for Catholics to take to the so-called 'war on terror' preoccupied me from 2002 through to the end of my time in Archbishop's House; and, finally, the issue that perhaps riled me more than any other – my disagreement with the government over Catholic adoption agencies. Each issue touched in a different way on the relationship between the Church and the public domain, either with the judiciary or with the government. And each was delicately poised, with good arguments on each side.

Basil Hume had been offered a peerage by three different prime ministers: James Callaghan, Margaret Thatcher and Tony Blair. He had always refused. But to my surprise, before he died he had a change of heart about bishops taking up seats in the House of Lords. He didn't want bishops or archbishops to be offered peerages at the personal whim of the prime minister. He now had a different idea up his sleeve.

In March 1999, a few months before his death, I was being driven down from the north of England, where I had been attending an event, when I had a telephone call from Basil. He had arranged a meeting at Archbishop's House at which ten members of Parliament were to be present, mostly peers, and eight or nine bishops.

'You're coming to this meeting tomorrow, aren't you?' he said.

I told him I was. 'Cormac, I want you to chair it, because I'm not up to it.'

What Basil wanted us to discuss was the possibility of Catholic bishops being given places in the House of Lords based on office rather than on the particular personality or profile of the individual. He told me that he didn't want to accept a life peerage as a sort of prize just because he had become a national figure. 'But', he added, 'what about the five Catholic archbishops sitting in the Lords, alongside the twenty-six Anglican bishops?'

I said, 'I think there might be something in that.'

We both knew that the House of Lords was likely to be reformed and that there would have to be a great deal of discussion and consultation before his proposal could be realized. But I shared his feeling that if there were to be Anglican bishops and other church leaders in whatever new arrangements were agreed, it would be helpful to have Catholic bishops there too, to add to the Christian voice, especially when laws with a moral dimension were being considered.

The peers at the meeting included Lord Hunt of Tamworth, Basil's brother-in-law, Lord Rees-Mogg, the former editor of *The Times*, and my old friend Norman St John-Stevas, now Lord St John of Fawsley; John Gummer, then still an MP, was also there. They were all keen on Basil's idea.

There were eight or nine bishops. We were split. There was an amusing exchange between Peter Smith and Pat Kelly. Peter said bluntly: 'I just don't agree, I don't think we should have Catholic bishops sitting in the Lords.' Pat said: 'We don't agree. What are we going to do?' He looked troubled. Peter said: 'It's all right, Patrick: it's not a matter of faith or morals. We are allowed to have different views sometimes.'

The discussion revealed an interesting fault line between the bishops. Some felt strongly that the Church was more effective as a voice from outside the establishment. There was a bit of working-class Catholicism in this, a sort of gut feeling that 'we don't want to be part of that lot'. Other bishops were more relaxed about it, feeling that we could have more effect on public policy and law-making if we were on the inside rather than the outside. They were all for rolling up their sleeves and entering the messy world of Parliament. They felt the presence of Catholic bishops in the Lords would in no way be opposed by our Anglican friends but that, on the contrary, most of them would welcome the addition of Catholic bishops as bolstering the Christian voice in Parliament. The peers at the meeting made the point that the Lords was less party political and more independent and representative of the people than the House of Commons, and they wanted voices from the hierarchy as well as lay Catholic voices there.

I could see both points of view, but on the whole I was in favour. I felt if Church of England bishops and other church leaders and people like the Chief Rabbi and some senior Muslim leaders were to be there, we should be there too, making our voice heard in the public square. But I recognized that there was also a practical consideration. As Peter Smith had said, 'We just haven't got the time'.

Afterwards I went in to see poor Basil, who was looking awful. I realized then how ill he was. It was a very awkward conversation. The meeting had been very much Basil's idea. It hadn't been something the other bishops had been pressing for. He asked: 'What did you decide?' I explained as tactfully as I could that it had been an interesting meeting. 'The Catholic peers and MPs were all very keen, but our people are a bit hesitant.' Basil still maintained his position, but it was left hanging in the air. He died a few months later.

Ten years later I was offered a place in the House of Lords by the then Prime Minister, Gordon Brown. In the meantime, George Carey, I remember, had been keen for me to be given a personal peerage; his idea was that the distinguished Muslim scholar, Zaki Badawi, the chief rabbi, Jonathan Sacks, and I would be made peers at the same time. In due course, Jonathan was appointed, which was of course the right thing to do. He is a very powerful presence in the House and his contribution has been quite invaluable.

I had some thinking to do before I could respond to the Prime Minister. I was in two minds. Remembering my conversations with Basil, part of me thought that it might be good for a Catholic archbishop to be in the House of Lords, where he might be able to make a contribution to debates on issues of social justice, or that affected the family or human dignity. It even crossed my mind that I could begin my opening speech with the words: 'As my predecessor in the House of Lords, Cardinal Reginald Pole, said in 1556 ...'!

But another part of me was much more hesitant. Not all our bishops would necessarily be in favour. And I could understand that it might be a little awkward for whoever my successor in Westminster would be to have the former cardinal archbishop in such a high-profile position in public life. I would also have to have the approval of Pope Benedict. Canon law states very clearly that clerics should not play any formal part in the government of their country, or take up political office.

In Rome, I explained to the pope that the House of Lords was quite distinct from the government and from party politics, in that it did not make laws but rather debated and, if necessary, amended them. He seemed open. I also had conversations with the secretary of state, Tarcisio Bertone, about it. They were obviously a bit torn. I took me several meetings in Rome before I could get a straight answer. Eventually, I was told: 'We've talked about it, and, well, we think more No than Yes.' There was the danger, which I understood, that it might set a precedent for church leaders in other parts of the world wanting to enter politics to say: 'Well, you allowed that bishop in England to take a seat in his parliament – why shouldn't I be allowed to run for president, or whatever?'

It was left to me make the decision, but I wrote to Gordon Brown to thank him for his kind invitation and explained that I was unable to accept it. Looking back now I'm rather glad not to have this responsibility. But I think Basil's idea is still quite a good one. If the House of Lords is to continue in anything like its current form, and if Church of England bishops keep their seats, or some of them, there might be a case for some Catholic and other religious leaders to have seats by virtue of their positions in their communities. Whatever plans they come up with for the reform of the House of Lords they certainly won't please everybody. I would be inclined to allow it to develop gradually, rather than making big, dramatic alterations. Keep some hereditary peers, add some elected peers, touch it up with more independent voices. Incremental change is usually best. But perhaps that's just Cormac, always the cautious reformer rather than the reckless revolutionary, talking.

The second issue was the heart-rending case of the twins who were known publicly at the time only as 'Jodie and Mary'. Their parents lived on the tiny island of Gozo, off the coast of Malta. An ultrasound scan before the birth of the twins revealed that they were conjoined in their mother's womb. The parents sought medical help in the United Kingdom, where further tests revealed that Jodie and Mary had only one functioning heart and set of lungs between them. One of the twins, they were told, was unlikely to survive the birth. The parents refused to contemplate the possibility of an abortion and on 8 August 2000 Jodie and Mary were born at St Mary's Hospital in Manchester by caesarean section.

Both the babies were very sick. Mary was only alive because of a shared artery. Her sister Jodie's health was rapidly deteriorating and was expected to fail by the time she was six months old if the twins remained conjoined. The doctors said that she had a very good chance of survival – but only if she was separated from her sister Mary. They asked the twins' mother and father for permission to operate. It was an agonizing decision for the parents. They had two daughters, and loved both of them. They refused to consent to the operation. As the mother explained, 'Why should we have to kill one of our daughters to enable the other one to survive?' They were content to place their faith in God and let his will decide the twins' future.

The doctors were also distraught. They were sure they could save the life of one of the twins in their care. They turned to the courts for permission to perform a surgical separation without parental consent. On 25 August a family court judge issued a judgement authorizing the doctors to perform the separation. The case went to a three-judge court of appeal. The court of appeal took an extraordinary step in asking me, as Archbishop of Westminster, to submit what is called an *amicus curiae* brief, outlining the moral issues in the case.

I outlined the traditional Catholic teaching that all human life is a gift from God. The life of each of the baby girls was sacred. No one should deliberately set out to cause an innocent person's death. Furthermore, there is no duty on a doctor to preserve life if doing so requires extraordinary measures or procedures that would result in a grave injustice. And it seemed clear to me that the deliberate killing of Mary would constitute such an injustice. I understood that it was a desperately difficult case. But I supported the parents in their opposition to allowing the doctors to separate their twin daughters.

The judges decided to allow the surgeons to operate, against the wishes of the parents, who chose not to take the case to the House of Lords. I could understand why they might have felt emotionally exhausted by what had been a long and arduous case. On 7 November a twenty-hour operation involving twenty-two medical staff was completed with only one certain result. Mary died on the operating table. Her parents left Jodie's bedside in Manchester and returned with Mary's body to Gozo, where she was laid to rest.

Some six or seven years later I was in Malta and I decided to pay a visit to Gozo to see the parents and the child. I was welcomed with great joy. I had never met the family before and it was good to see the parents and of course 'Jodie', whose real name was Gracie Attard. She was a delightful child, and I understand that she is now a lively teenager, with ambitions to be a doctor. Her mother told me that she would need to have many more operations. And there would always be the trauma of the separation from her sister, whose life had to be sacrificed so that she might live.

It was a tragic and heart-rending case. Seeing Gracie playing happily with her friends made me feel thankful that she was alive. I understand why the judges made the decision they did. Everyone concerned with the case, the parents, the doctors and nurses, the judges, wanted to act for the best. But I am haunted by the thought that a very dangerous precedent might have been set in English law that could allow an innocent person lawfully to be killed or lethally assaulted. It is a case I still turn over in my mind.

The third issue has touched almost all of us, directly or indirectly. It was the war in Iraq, which finally began, after several months of mounting tension, with the invasion of Iraq by the armed forces of the United States, the United Kingdom and their allies in March 2003.

Like many others at the time, I thought and reflected deeply on the morality of the war. In the period during which a military attack on the Saddam Hussein regime was being considered, I asked three distinguished Catholic public figures to help me make up my mind as to what might be the right thing to say or to write. We met around a table in Archbishop's House: Lord Guthrie, a distinguished soldier and retired chief of the defence staff; and two civil servants, Sir David Goodall, a former high commissioner to India, and the late Sir Michael Quinlan, the former permanent secretary at the ministry of defence.

My mind went back to the general synod of bishops that had met in Rome shortly after 11 September 2001. Bishops from every quarter of the globe immediately conveyed their heartfelt sympathy to the bishops of the United States, and through them to the American people, at the appalling loss of life in the attack on the World Trade Center. I was struck, though, by a recognition that for many of the bishops in the developing world, conflict and war, and the atrocity of the unnecessary and avoidable loss of life through poverty and disease, were matters of everyday life. Hundreds of thousands had been slaughtered in Rwanda in 1994, with no effective response from the international community. They had been living with slaughter and hunger and premature death for generations, while the rest of the world was paying no attention.

So my personal instinct was that the best response to the atrocities in New York was not to put our energy and resources into a 'war on terror', as it was being called. I was concerned that military intervention would set the Arab world against the West, and undermine the already slender hopes for peace between Israel and the Palestinian people. What we needed was not a war on terror but a war on its underlying cause. There will be no peace in our world without justice.

I wrote in *The Times* in September 2002:

There are occasions when a short-term response to an imminent threat serves an important preventive purpose. However, the problems of our planet cannot be solved by unilateral military action alone. In a globalised world the wisdom of specific actions or policies in international impact must ultimately be judged by the extent to which they improve the lot of all mankind, especially the poorest, and enhance the prospect for world peace. At present there are genuine reasons to doubt that military action against Iraq would pass that test.

I rang Rowan Williams. We found ourselves on the same wavelength, and in the days leading up to the invasion we issued a joint statement reiterating our doubts about the moral legitimacy as well as the unpredictable humanitarian consequences of a war with Iraq.

To some extent, Basil's time in office were the Thatcher years. Mine were the years of Tony Blair and Gordon Brown, the years of New Labour. In 2000, when I became archbishop, Blair was in his heyday. I used to see Tony and Cherie in Downing Street occasionally, and sometimes at Chequers. Tony was always rather more anxious to talk about theology than politics. He used to ask me about the Bible and the Qur'an, and about Catholic social teaching, He was genuinely fascinated by religion. He asked me once what I thought about Muslim schools. If Roman Catholics and Anglicans were able to have their own schools then it seemed logical for other faith communities to have their schools too. I didn't disagree, but I told him there would be the danger of creating a divided community unless there was a firm insistence across all the faith schools, Christian, Jewish or Muslim, on common citizenship and shared values. I received him into the Catholic Church at Archbishop's House in December 2007, six months or so after he left office.

Gordon Brown stands very high in my estimation. He was, of course, the son of a Church of Scotland minister. He was always gracious and eager to chat. We used to talk about rugby: he had been a keen player until he had suffered an injury as a schoolboy that nearly cost him his sight. Brown's commitment to the poor, both at home and in the developing world, is utterly genuine. When I invited him to a meeting of senior bishops in Rome to discuss global poverty and the millennium goals, he gladly came. He impressed everyone by the passion of his commitment to the poor and by the force and logic of his arguments. Tackling poverty, disease and injustice in the poorest countries is the great moral issue of our time. Again, I go back to the basic truth that there will be no true peace in the world without the elimination of dire poverty.

Finally, the issue that most infuriated me: the struggle with the government over Catholic adoption agencies.

In April 2007, the regulations of the Equality Act (sexual orientation) came into effect. They made discrimination in the provision of goods, facilities and services on the grounds of sexual orientation illegal. This was to have the unintended consequence of leading to the closure of Catholic adoption agencies which had been doing excellent work, finding good homes for some of the most vulnerable young children in society.

Because of our conviction that children are better placed in a home with a father and mother, the Catholic agencies were unable to offer a service to same-sex couples. Of course, the Church didn't have a problem about legislation to outlaw unjust discrimination against gay people. The argument wasn't about that. I simply felt strongly that there should be a space for Catholic adoption agencies to be allowed to continue their traditional policy of placing children in homes where they would have a father and mother.

We sought an exception to be made to the legislation that would allow these few small religious voluntary agencies – which made up only 4 per cent of the sector – to continue their work. This would not in any way have denied gay couples access to mainstream providers of adoption services. It seemed to me that this would have been a sensible accommodation, recognizing that religious organizations had a distinct identity and ethos, and allowing these adoption agencies to continue making a valuable contribution to the wider common good of society.

I spoke to Tony Blair on the phone about it. He was sympathetic. I think he knew I was right. But he was coming to the end of his time as Prime Minister and he no longer had the same clout around the cabinet table. He had to pick his fights, and I got the impression that he didn't feel he could afford to squander political capital on the defence of Catholic adoption agencies against the intimidating forces of political correctness. Of course, once an equality law is passed, governments don't like giving exemptions from it, I understand that. Personally, looking back, I'm sorry I didn't take the issue to the High Court.

It was one of the rare occasions when I felt angry. It seemed to me that this was all about putting gesture politics before the interests of children. The government didn't need to do it. That was the annoying thing. It seemed extraordinary to me that a law, in the name of tolerance, should become so intolerant that it ended up forcing charities that aim only to do good and foster the most vulnerable children to close down. It was unfair and totally unnecessary.

It was also difficult for me because it created some disharmony among the bishops. We usually worked well together, and were able to disagree as friends. It was one of the things I was proudest of. But on this issue there were certainly raised voices. Some thought we should continue to look for some sort of compromise; some felt on this issue we had to oppose the government head-on. Some felt the agencies should just carry on as before and wait to see what would happen. But most felt the new legislation made the position of Catholic adoption agencies untenable. In the end, some of the agencies changed their name and broke their link with the Church; others closed.

I admire our pluralist society, but in my view we have to strike a much fairer balance, which recognizes the importance of religion and belief and allows a more open and mature accommodation of differences while ensuring that the law prevents harm and protects everyone equally.

14

Awkward corners

I'd first met Cardinal Basil Hume while I was rector of the English College in Rome and was looking for someone to act as a spiritual director for the students. Gordon Wheeler, Bishop of Leeds, had told me that the Abbot of Ampleforth would be helpful, so I arranged to spend a few days at the monastery in north Yorkshire. We had several conversations, covered a lot of ground and got on together very well. Basil was extraordinarily open with me about all his troubles, even though he had never met me before. Being abbot had become a real struggle and in some ways he was very glad to go to Westminster. He told me later that he found being Cardinal Archbishop of Westminster, at least for the early years, considerably easier than being Abbot of Ampleforth.

I admired Basil's spirituality – I still turn to *Searching for God* for spiritual reading – his intelligence, his *savoir-faire*. He had a natural air of authority and of goodness, a presence that impressed itself on all who met him. He became a much-loved national figure and managed to leave us feeling that the Catholic Church had become a central part of British life rather than something peripheral to it.

Basil's strength and appeal to so many rested, I think, in his manifest Benedictine spirituality. This was something British people had not witnessed before and to see it clearly in the presence and life of the Archbishop of Westminster was very powerful. He could also be good fun. I remember once going up to see him about something or another, and suddenly he said: 'Come on, Cormac, let's go and watch the match on the box instead.' It was an Ireland v. England game; we both thought we knew more about rugby than the commentators so we turned the volume down and provided our own expert summaries.

Cardinal Basil had an apartment at the top of Archbishop's House which he called his 'cell'. When I moved in we went back to an arrangement that I think was what the architect originally intended, with my rooms on the same floor as the large reception room and the archbishop's office. I'd had a lovely house in Storrington which I was sorry to leave, and it felt a bit strange moving to London. I'd lived in Rome, of course, but in England I'd always lived in large towns: Reading, Portsmouth, Southampton. Living in the heart of London was different altogether. I missed the greenery. I used to walk around Vincent Square most days; I loved St James' Park, but it was nearly a mile away.

There was a sense in which Basil was always the abbot. He was very keen on obedience. I was, perhaps, more collegial at bishops' conferences. I think we both enjoyed the company of the bishops and our conferences together were congenial affairs. Basil used to chair our bishops' meetings very well, though I had the feeling he usually wanted them to end as quickly as possible. I always enjoyed the opportunity of meeting for a few days with the other bishops. They were a mixed bunch but I liked them all and found working with them a real pleasure.

I'm not really a worrier. I tend to think things will work out for the best. I always like to have a sense of where I want to take things, but I can be inclined to wing it a bit. I'm not always, I have to admit, a master of detail. So I've always looked to have people around me who are able to go through things line by line, who will pick up on things I might miss. I was very lucky with the people I had advising me: Andrew Summersgill, Charles Wookey, Tim Livesey, Stephen Wall, Austen Ivereigh, John Gibbs and, later on, Alexander DesForges and Maggie Doherty.

I could push things through when I felt sure something needed doing. I consulted the priests of the archdiocese before I dropped the area system instituted in Basil's time. The majority of them told me they'd prefer to leave things as they were. They liked having their own area bishop, their own little mini-diocese. I decided to change it anyway. But on the whole, my touch was probably lighter.

Among the bishops, Peter Smith took care of the social work agenda; Vincent picked up and ran with schools, and the way he took forward the practicalities of seeing through the Nolan Report is something for which I will always be grateful. Basil had increasingly come to rely on Vincent when he was his auxiliary, and I began to appreciate why.

Basil and I both had our occasional differences with Rome. We'd both said vaguely provocative things about the possibility of ordaining married men to the priesthood. When I told him, 'I've been sent this letter from Rome about what I said about married clergy', he said, 'Yes! I've had one too'. He reacted strongly. 'I'll tell you what, Cormac,' he said, 'why don't we go to Rome and we'll confront them? We'll go together and sort this out.'

Cardinal Basil wasn't really comfortable in Rome at all, and some people in Rome weren't really comfortable with him either, just as they weren't really comfortable with Cardinal Bergoglio. In 1980, after the National Pastoral Congress in Liverpool, Derek and Basil had gone out to Rome, where they spoke at the synod of bishops on the family. Derek talked about finding a way back to communion for people who had been divorced and remarried, and Basil tried to open up a little space for development of the teaching in *Humanae Vitae* about the ban of artificial means of contraception. He made a lovely speech about a 'dream', in which the pilgrim church was limping along a road, following weather-beaten signposts on which the paint was fading. When they met later privately, Pope John Paul said to him: 'Keep dreaming.'

I was different, I suppose. I knew Rome better, and was more relaxed about their little ways. Perhaps I was more compliant. I was certainly exasperated by unnecessary meddling sometimes or a general tendency to get the wrong end of the stick. But I couldn't complain that the curia was breathing down my neck all the time. In some ways, they would be quite meticulous. A bishop was a bishop. It's a very minor point, but here's an example: when Pope John Paul came to Britain in 1982, I said to Basil, 'You must meet him when he arrives; you're the boss', but Basil told me, 'No. He's arriving into Gatwick; it's in your diocese, and I've been told you must greet him'. They are uncomfortable with big hierarchies, the Americans and the Brazilians with their huge bishops' conferences. Much easier to deal with bishops one at a time.

Once or twice as archbishop, I had to say to the head of a congregation in Rome, 'You must let me deal with that. But give me a little time, don't rush me', and normally they didn't. I used to go round the various congregations in Rome once a year at least, so when problems did arise, at least I was a familiar face.

When I took over, there were serious differences between the English-speaking cardinals and the congregation in Rome responsible for liturgy and worship over the new translation of the liturgy. The process was not mutually helpful. It contributed to an increased sense of irritation and lack of confidence between the periphery of the Church and the centre during my nine years at Westminster.

After Pablo Puente retired as the papal nuncio in 2003, we had another Spaniard, Faustino Sainz Muñoz, and I used to go and see him occasionally. We'd meet and we'd go for a walk on Wimbledon Common, and we would talk very freely. The appointment of bishops was never far away from the top of our agenda. I would always be consulted, but although I could suggest the names of people I thought would make good bishops (and occasionally suggest the names of people who wouldn't), I didn't have the final word. The nuncio consulted widely and all views about future bishops were taken into account.

One of the trickiest corners I had to negotiate with Rome was over the so-called 'Soho Masses'. A group had been organizing a Mass intended to be especially welcoming to gay Catholics and their families and friends since 1999. Several priests had agreed to celebrate at these Masses, including people whom I respected very much, and who assured me that the Masses were not rallies for campaigners or platforms for preachers to challenge Church teaching on homosexuality. I got the impression they were pretty much like an ordinary parish Mass, except that the music tended to be rather better. But it was an irregular situation: the services were held in an Anglican church, St Anne's in Soho, and were dependent on the goodwill of the Anglican Bishop of London and the local vicar. And a lot of people were insisting that the Masses were wrong and had to be stopped.

Usually, it's best for a bishop to solve pastoral problems in his diocese without seeking Vatican approval first, but in this case my instinct was that we should make sure we had the tacit approval of the key figures in Rome before we acted, otherwise I knew there could be trouble down the line. So I met the prefect of the Congregation for the Doctrine of the Faith to see if I could hammer out an acceptable solution. Fortunately for me, from 2005, when Joseph Ratzinger was elected pope, this was

William Levada. He was sympathetic. Levada had previously been Archbishop of San Francisco, and had personal experience of a similar situation.

While I was dealing with the CDF in Rome, one of my auxiliary bishops in Westminster was meeting with the group organizing the Masses. It was delicate. There were some prickly customers on each side. Levada leaned over backwards to be helpful, but it was at a time when there were people in Rome who seemed to enjoy stirring up trouble. It would be different now I think. Many homosexuals felt ostracized by the Church, and these Masses had become a route back to the sacraments for many Catholics who had become estranged from their faith.

We finally reached an understanding that the Masses would continue, moving from the Anglican church in Soho to the Catholic church of Our Lady of the Assumption on Warwick Street; at the same time we issued a statement on this ministry to homosexual Catholics that made it clear that the Church's teaching was not to be opposed or confused. The pressure to close down these Masses continued and after I retired, Vincent wisely moved the Masses away from Warwick Street, which he gave to the Ordinariate as their London base. The group was integrated into one of the regular Masses held at the Jesuit church in Farm Street, Mayfair. Perhaps my approach had been right at the time; in retrospect, I think Vincent handled the matter more deftly than I did.

One of the things I was keen to do as archbishop was to help get a conversation going about religion in society, to reconnect the Church to the public square at a time when our culture seemed to me to be becoming increasingly materialistic and secularized. I hosted two series of public lectures in the cathedral, one on the relationship between Europe and the Christian faith and the other on the role of faith in contemporary Britain. The capacity of the cathedral is about 2,000, so I was slightly nervous that we might end up delivering our talks to rows of empty seats. I asked Mary McAleese, Chris Patten, Timothy Radcliffe, Jean Vanier and Bob Geldof to take part in the first series, and then three years later I was joined by Tony Blair, Mark Thompson, Rowan Williams, William Hague and Julia Neuberger.

I was worried up to the last minute that Bob Geldof wouldn't show up. It always seemed a little implausible to imagine him behind a lectern in Westminster Cathedral. I'd asked him a year in advance and he'd said, 'Sure', but then he had second thoughts and tried to get out of it. I told him it had been publicized everywhere, he had to come. In the end he was as good as his word. When we entered the cathedral and were making our way to the front of the audience, I whispered in his ear: 'Now, Bob, no swearing.' The cathedral was full. 'I'm not used to speaking to such a small crowd ...' he began. I thought we might be in for an evening of one-liners. But then he went on to give one of the most serious and thought-provoking lectures of the series.

I was delighted to see, each week, the cathedral packed with people, including many who had never darkened the door of a Catholic church before, who had come to listen to speakers exploring the role of religion in society.

I came to love London, and there was nowhere else I seriously considered living when I retired in 2009. It seems to me that there is something especially 'catholic' about the way London holds together people of so many very different social and ethnic backgrounds. On 1 May 2006 we had the first May Day Mass for migrants in the cathedral. It was one of those occasions when I felt the gospel spring into life in all its vibrancy and generosity. As well as the papal nuncio and the Archbishop of Southwark, I concelebrated with more than fifty priests from London's ethnic chaplaincies. There was music from Africa, Latin America and Poland, and readings and prayers in Filipino, Malayalam, Lebanese, Spanish, Lithuanian and Chinese.

I don't think I've ever known the cathedral to be quite so packed. There were certainly illegal immigrants and asylum seekers among the congregation, and my homily had a political edge to it – I called for the government to consider an amnesty for illegal immigrants who had been here for some time – but the main purpose of the Mass was to let these groups know that they were valued and welcome. There were tears, I remember, when I said: 'As far as the Catholic Church is concerned, you are all Londoners. We want you to feel welcome in our parishes and our schools and our ethnic chaplaincies. We want you to know that you belong.'

In January 2002, I was invited by the Queen to spend a weekend at Sandringham and to preach at the Sunday morning service. Apart from myself there were four or five other guests, as well as Prince Philip and Sophie, Countess of Wessex. I drove up to Norfolk from London on the Saturday afternoon and was greeted on arrival by the Queen and Prince Philip. At dinner that evening I asked her when she would pay a visit to Ireland. She told me that she would love to go to Ireland but that 'they' – her advisors, I presumed – had cautioned against it. I was delighted when, nine years later, she was finally able to make her historic visit to Ireland and was received with great joy and acclaim.

I got up early the next morning so that I could celebrate Mass at a nearby Catholic church before going on to the local church in Sandringham for the Morning Service. I had prepared my sermon with a little more care than usual. I had expected that I might be preaching with the Queen and Prince Philip in front of me, but in fact they were sitting behind me in the choir. The Prince was thoughtful enough to make a few comments over lunch, so I knew he at least hadn't nodded off to sleep. He could rarely resist making a few digs at church teaching.

After dinner on the Sunday evening, the Queen asked me if I had enjoyed my weekend. 'Was there anything at all that did not work out as you would have wished?' Of course it had been a wonderful treat, as you'd expect, but I told her that I'd been asked to bring casual clothes, so I had been to Pinks on Jermyn Street and had bought myself a new check shirt and a pair of corduroy trousers. She leaned over to Prince Philip and said: 'Oh dear, the poor Cardinal has got himself new clothes for the barbecue which we had to cancel because of the awful weather.'

When I came down the next morning, bacon and eggs were laid out for us to help ourselves. The Queen never comes down for breakfast, and the others must have pushed off. There was just Prince Philip and myself. The morning papers were all laid out and I was curious to see if there were any pictures of me with the Queen. But the only royal story that morning was about Prince Harry, who was in the soup about something or other. The Prince and I looked at each other and shrugged. I drove home with my new check shirt still in its wrapper.

Pope Francis asked me if I could join them when he met the Queen on her visit to Rome in April 2014. Of course I agreed, but protocol wouldn't allow it. He was a tiny bit nervous, not like him. Popes are used to a stream of visitors, royalty, presidents and all the rest of it, but there's something special about meeting the Queen of England, even for a pope.

I remember the late Queen Mother with great affection. We sat together once at a lunch given by Lord St John-Stevas and we were talking about the war and then we started to sing the songs we both remembered: 'We'll meet again', 'A Nightingale Sang in Berkeley Square' and 'The White Cliffs of Dover'. Then she suddenly said: 'I wonder if you know this one?' It was called, I think, 'Taxi' – and she sang it, very sweetly. I told her I thought I knew all the songs of the Second World War but I had never heard of that one. 'You wouldn't,' she said, 'it was a hit tune in 1910.' That was the last time I saw her.

I have met Prince Charles on many occasions and always enjoyed our conversations. I admire his dedication, his courage in adversity and his wholehearted desire to serve the common good in different ways. As someone said recently on the radio, 'the world would be a poorer place without him'.

A few months before my 75th birthday in August 2007, I wrote to offer my resignation to Pope Benedict, as required by canon law. I received a letter back from Rome asking me to continue *'donec aliter provideatur'* ('until otherwise provided for'). They saw me staying on for another three or four years. But I thought one year would be enough, though in fact I remained on for nearly two years. I felt not so much that I'd done my bit and deserved a rest – I actually found myself enjoying the job the more I got the hang of it, and a part of me would have liked to have gone on for a few more years – but that it would be best for me to let go. I'd had a troubled reign, took a bit of a battering, survived, more or less … and now that the storms had subsided perhaps somebody with a clean bill of health should be given a crack at it. And I didn't want to spend two years listening to people speculating about who was going to follow me.

I had suggested to her secretary that I would like to invite the Queen to Archbishop's House before I left, perhaps for a brief visit. I didn't hear anything, but then I rang Lord Camoys, who had been Lord Chamberlain. 'Oh,' he said, 'leave it to me.' Soon afterwards, he came back to me and said: 'Yes, she'd be delighted to visit you. She'll come to lunch.'

She came with Prince Philip. They arrived bang on time, at ten to one. We had a reception in the throne room for about seventy – I had invited people I'd worked closely with to a little leaving party, but I only told them that morning that they would be meeting the Queen – and then we went in to a small private lunch, just myself, Sr Clement and Sr Damian, the nuncio, Faustino Sainz Muñoz, and the auxiliary bishops. I sat the Queen next to Sr Clement and they got on like a house on fire, talking about horses. I will always be grateful to her for her gracious gesture in accepting my invitation.

There were several lovely farewell parties, but the one I remember best was a long, long lunch at the end of one of the final meetings I had as president of the bishops' conference. All of them said a few words. I was touched and, of course, felt just a little sad. And it was all a little strange. There had been nine previous Cardinal Archbishops of Westminster, but I had been the first to live to tell the tale.

15

'Watch out!'

I sometimes wonder if I was asked to join the Congregation for Bishops as a sort of consolation prize after deciding not to take up Gordon Brown's offer of a seat in the House of Lords. I understood the concern in Rome that it might set a precedent for prelates in other parts of the world who might want to stand for political office. But what had really swayed my decision was that my fellow bishops were divided about the wisdom of having an Emeritus Cardinal Archbishop in such a prominent public role. I could understand their hesitation. The decision was left to me, but they were pleased in Rome that I elected not to take up Brown's offer. And then I learned from Cardinal Bertone in October 2009 that I had been appointed to two congregations in Rome.

The Congregation for Bishops is responsible for recommending bishops' appointments to the pope for dioceses in Europe and the Americas and elsewhere. My other new job in Rome was to be a member of the Congregation for the Evangelization of Peoples, formerly known as Propaganda Fidei, which recommends bishops for so-called 'mission territories', which are mostly in Africa and Asia. Between them, these two congregations discussed and recommended to the pope nearly two hundred appointments every year.

The Congregation for Bishops met in Rome twice a month, usually over a Thursday morning. There were between twenty and thirty cardinals and archbishops at each session, most of whom lived in Rome. I joined them for some of their meetings, and it involved a lot of travelling. On my retirement I had moved to Chiswick, which was very handy for Heathrow. I was able to help out the parish priest of Our Lady of Grace and St Edward on Chiswick High Road. I didn't have a lot of personal belongings to bring with me. Some books, a few pictures, and the piano I bought in 1966 when I went to work with Derek. As a priest, you get used to moving on.

In the selection of bishops, much depends on the apostolic nuncio. For each appointment, the nuncio's job is to prepare a list of three candidates – the *terna* – for the congregation to consider. If you have a good nuncio then he has consulted widely and has put a good dossier on all three candidates together, with his recommendation noted but leaving the congregation with a genuine choice. The nuncios we had in the UK in my time were very good. I enjoyed working with Pablo Puente, a shrewd and intelligent man. London was his last post and he was perhaps inclined to think that having appointed me as Archbishop of Westminster he could sit back a bit. I much enjoyed working with Faustino Sainz Muñoz, who followed him in 2004. He was diligent in going around the country and taking soundings, not only from the archbishops and bishops but from priests and lay people in the diocese. The present nuncio, my friend Antonio Mennini, arrived after I had retired.

We had perhaps four appointments on our agenda each time we met. One of us would be chosen to summarize all the documentation and to present a summary to the others. After hearing this cardinal's report, we would discuss the appointment and then take a vote. Sometimes we followed the recommendation of the nuncio; sometimes we picked another of the candidates on the *terna*; and sometimes we asked the nuncio to come back with a new list of three candidates.

Some time after we'd come to a conclusion, the cardinal prefect would present our findings to Pope Benedict. He was, of course, free to do what he wanted. I'd say nine times out of ten, he accepted the name we had recommended; sometimes, he chose one of the other two names on the *terna*. And occasionally, he rejected all three names and asked for a fresh *terna*. He could even pick somebody else. The congregation then notifed the nuncio of the pope's decision, and he would contact the candidate.

In preparing our recommendations for the pope, the orthodoxy of the candidate was vital. You couldn't have a bishop who was unsure on certain aspects of church teaching. And you had to be careful about matching the right man to a particular diocese. Probably not a good idea to appoint a Basque to Madrid. As I sat there, I tried to imagine the meeting at which the 45-year-old Cormac Murphy-O'Connor had been discussed as a possible new bishop for Arundel and Brighton. There were no black marks against my name, apparently: good Catholic family, three brothers in the priesthood, rector of the English College. I had never published anything in a theological journal that might raise an eyebrow and nothing I'd said as a priest or as a rector seems to have provoked the protectors of orthodoxy to have written a letter of complaint to Rome behind my back. Somebody told me later: 'I've never seen such a clean sheet.' As I've mentioned, things were a little more complicated twenty-three years later when the vacancy at Westminster was being considered. By that time, my file was a little fuller.

Sometimes good priests are blocked from becoming bishops because of a complaint to Rome against them. A complaint about a priest should first be dealt with at a local level, where the decision should be made as to its seriousness or otherwise, and whether or not it should be referred to Rome. When complaints are made over the local bishop's head and sent direct to Rome, they should automatically be returned to be dealt with locally, and then forwarded with comment to the appropriate congregation in Rome.

It may have crossed my mind that I had been asked to join the congregation to cheer me up and keep me busy and useful now that I wouldn't be sitting in Parliament. But there was a more serious reason. Giovanni Battista Re, the cardinal prefect of the congregation, suggested that I might bring more harmony and balance to the discussion of appointments in English-speaking countries. In June 2010, when he passed his 80th birthday, Marc Ouellet, a Canadian from Quebec, took over as prefect. Soon after he was elected, Pope Francis made changes at the congregation; I was delighted that after I had reached 80, as well as being made cardinal, Vincent was also appointed to this congregation.

The English can fight when they have to. But they don't go out of their way to look for a scrap. We're not by nature culture warriors. My impression is that this temperament – pragmatic rather than ideological – appeals to Pope Francis. I'm starting to notice more Englishmen in senior positions in Rome nowadays.

In the early Church, bishops were elected by the local clergy and lay people and only later on did their choice have to be approved by the senior bishop of the area. In the medieval period, more power was given to (or grabbed by) the local rulers and kings, who gradually came to decide who would be installed as bishop. It is only comparatively recently that the present way of appointing bishops was established. There's no perfect way of selecting bishops. If we went back to leaving it entirely to the local church, there would be a danger of archbishops and bishops' conferences choosing like-minded men who wouldn't rock the boat. However, having seen how the current system works both as an archbishop and as a member of the Congregation for Bishops, I am inclined to think that more weight should be given to the local bishops' conference. They know the particular needs of a diocese best, and they are in the best position to judge the candidate who would be the best fit. If bishops are to govern the Church – always with the pope – their role in choosing fellow bishops should be given more focus and attention. But on the whole the present system is fair and just.

I learnt that there is no one definition of what makes an 'ideal bishop'. There are different sorts of men who are right for different times and different places. And a good bishops' conference should have a sprinkling of different characters and temperaments: some who are quick on their feet and want to hurry to a decision, some who insist on time to reflect; some who might bend a little, some who are a little stiff; some teachers, some scholars, perhaps an accountant, maybe even a saint. I realized how fortunate I had been with the bishops around me. We didn't always agree about everything, but when we argued, it was as friends, and there was very little difficulty when someone didn't get their own way. I came to realize that in other bishops' conferences, the normal differences you find in any group sometimes came close to divisiveness.

On 11 February 2013, Pope Benedict announced that he had decided to retire. It was, of course, a great surprise; but it was not a complete shock. On an earlier visit to Rome, there'd been a few whispers that he would resign, but I hadn't quite believed it. Not since 1294 had a pope resigned voluntarily and it was always felt that any pope would remain in office until his death. It is said that Benedict had laid flowers on the tomb of St Celestine when he visited Aquila in July 2010. Perhaps that should have given us a clue. Celestine, a hermit monk, had only accepted the papacy reluctantly, and he resigned after just five months.

I remember Benedict with admiration and affection. As well as several instances of personal kindness, I have a special reason to be grateful to him. When I retired in 2009 and had to pack up my belongings to move from Westminster to Chiswick, I had to go through my library and decide which of my books I could not be parted from. I was reminded of how many of Joseph Ratzinger's theological works and homilies and addresses I had accumulated over the years, and how often I had turned to them for their teaching, for their insight and for their encouragement.

His early book, *Introduction to Christianity*, is still among the most convincing summaries of the basics of the faith. I have often recommended it to people looking for an intellectually stretching but accessible account of what we believe as Catholics. To have written a work of biblical scholarship as accomplished as *Jesus of Nazareth* while serving as pope was an astonishing achievement. His homilies, easy to read, deeply spiritual, have been helpful to me – I admit I have plagiarized them more than once – and to many other priests too. When his two encyclical letters on Love and Hope, *Deus Caritas Est* and *Spe Salvi*, arrived in the post, I read them first out of duty – cardinals must keep up with what the pope is teaching – but then with growing appreciation and pleasure. They are great encyclicals. Rarely, if ever, has the Church had a pope who could convey the teachings of the Gospel so clearly and attractively, who could be both so readable and so profound.

So there was no hesitation. All his books came with me. For as long as I am able to pick up a book I will turn to them for nourishment, and I will think of the man who wrote them with respect, fondness and gratitude. I am glad to think of Benedict quietly living out his days in some ease and comfort, reading and studying quietly and praying for his beloved Church.

Many of the challenges and difficulties that Benedict had to face when he was elected pope in 2005 had originated in the previous years, when Pope John Paul had become frail and ill. The Vatican in those years had lacked a sense of direction and Benedict, as he admitted himself, was not given to strong and directive management. Many of the people around him, in my view, were simply not up to the job. In the years that followed his election the Vatican lapsed further into a state of disarray, which was gradually felt throughout the Catholic world. The attacks on the Catholic Church for its failure to protect children from abuse by priests and to deal swiftly and firmly with the perpetrators, which had in earlier years been directed at the bishops of local churches, now became increasingly directed at the Vatican and at Benedict personally. Everything seemed to be going wrong and I felt deeply sorry for him.

We in Britain will remember Benedict particularly for his visit in September 2010, the first-ever state visit by a pope to the United Kingdom. He had not been getting a very good press before the visit and Vincent – who had succeeded me as Archbishop of Westminster the previous year – and I went to see him to brief him about the condition of the Church in our country and to talk about some of the things that it might be important for him to say. On both sides, as well as excitement at the prospect of his visit, there was a little nervousness about the reception he would receive.

On the flight over from Rome, Benedict spoke frankly to journalists of the shame and sorrow he had felt as he had learnt about the abuse of children by Catholic priests. He could not understand, he said, 'how a priest, who at the moment of ordination says "yes" to Christ, in order to be his mouth, his hand and to serve him with all his being, could abuse children'. He admitted freely that the Church's leadership had not responded quickly enough or decisively enough. This is, he said, 'a time of penance, a time of humility; we must renew and learn again absolute sincerity. Our first interest must be the victims; how to repair the damage, how to assist these persons in overcoming their trauma, in finding life again, in finding again trust in the message of Christ.'

The greeting by the Duke of Edinburgh on his landing at Edinburgh airport, and then the kind and warm exchanges between the pope and the Queen at the reception at Holyrood Palace, seemed to set the tone for the whole visit. Afterwards we all went on for a lunch hosted at his home by the then Archbishop of Edinburgh, Cardinal Keith O'Brien; it was, I think, the first time that a pope had tasted haggis. He was well up to it, and later enjoyed the tumultuous greetings of thousands of Scots lining the streets of Edinburgh, cheering and waving flags in the sunshine, before being driven to Bellahouston Park, Glasgow, where he celebrated Mass on the feast of St Ninian.

Although I was retired, at Vincent's insistence I was part of the small party that travelled with the pope. The success of the visit surprised everyone. Here was the pope who had been mocked as 'God's Rottweiler' being seen as a humble, gentle, good man, a shepherd concerned only for the good of his flock. A high point was his address in Westminster Hall to 'civil society'. Politicians, diplomats, academics and business leaders – among them Margaret Thatcher, John Major, Tony Blair and Gordon Brown – listened intently to what the pope had to say. It was a *tour de force*, an intelligent and thought-provoking reflection on the place of religion in contemporary society. He reached out for common ground between faith and reason, between Christianity and the state. I remember feeling particularly happy to hear him say that religion is not a problem for legislators to solve but a vital contributor to the national conversation. It would be disastrous if religion, particularly Christianity, were in any way marginalized in our society.

Later that afternoon, I sat near Pope Benedict at the ecumenical service at Westminster Abbey, where he was visibly impressed by the magnificent liturgy. My mind went back to the visit of Pope John Paul to Canterbury Cathedral during his pastoral visit of 1982. My heart had been filled with hope that day and I was moved to see his successor as pope returning to us as a pilgrim from Rome twenty-eight years later, praying before the tomb of St Edward the Confessor, and, in spite of all the difficulties and obstacles, urging us to keep faith with the ecumenical journey. 'Our commitment to Christian unity', he reminded us, 'is born of nothing less than our faith in Christ.'

Nor can I easily forget the Mass at Crofton Park on the final day of his visit, at which Cardinal John Henry Newman was beatified. Benedict's heartfelt connection to Newman and his work was clear. He was delighted that he had been able to come in person to Birmingham to bestow on this much-loved father of soul the Church's solemn recognition of his outstanding holiness. The bishops then had a final meeting with the pope at Oscott College before he left for the airport, where in a parting speech, the Prime Minister, David Cameron, acknowledged that he had reminded all of us of the vital role that Christians play in society. 'You have really challenged the whole country', he said, 'to sit up and think.'

Before he entered his plane, Benedict turned and gave a final, shy wave. I know he treasured the days he spent with us, as we did with him, and that he carried back many happy memories with him to Rome.

I am sure that he had been thinking about his resignation for quite a long time. 'Old age and weakness', he said, 'played the major part in my decision.' He felt keenly that the challenges facing the Church were steadily mounting and I think he knew in his heart that he no longer had the strength or the energy to confront them. It was a very brave decision, and in making it, Pope Benedict was thinking primarily of the good of the Church. The date of the resignation was set for Thursday 28 February 2013, which would give an opportunity for the new pope to be in office before the ceremonies of Holy Week and Easter.

I arrived in Rome on Wednesday 27 February. I was very moved by Benedict's words at his final public audience in St Peter's Square that afternoon. He talked about his pilgrim path, which had seen joy and light but had also had its difficult moments. And he spoke of how he had felt:

> like Peter with the apostles in the boat on the sea of Galilee: the Lord has given us so many days of sun and of light winds, days when the catch was abundant; there were also moments when the waters were rough and the winds were against us, just as it has always been throughout the Church's history, and when the Lord seemed to be sleeping. But I have always known that the Lord is in that boat, and I have always known that the barque of the Church is not mine but his. Nor does the Lord let it sink.

He went on: 'My heart is filled with gratitude to God, for never did he leave the Church, or me personally, without his consolation, his light, his love.' It was a reminder of Benedict's adroitness with words; his final address was one of his most beautiful.

The next day, along with the other cardinals I met Benedict for the last time as pope in the marbled Clementine Hall of the Vatican's

Apostolic Palace. One by one we each went up and greeted him and thanked him for all he had done, each of us assuring him that we would always pray with him and for him. He then spoke to us for the last time as Supreme Pontiff of the Catholic Church. He was gentle and kind; and that is how I will always remember him. In the afternoon I watched his departure by helicopter to his temporary residence at Castel Gandolfo. It was all very strange and very moving. What did the Lord have in store for his Church?

The conclave of 2013 was like no other. There was no funeral to be discussed and planned, and therefore when the cardinals gathered on Monday 4 March in the synod hall for the first of the general congregations, we had a whole week to talk together about the challenges and hopes for the future. As in the days after the death of Pope John Paul eight years earlier, we met twice each day, in the morning and then again in the evening. All 151 cardinals, including those like me who were over 80 and therefore would not be entering the conclave to elect Benedict's successor, were present at these meetings.

By now, I knew Jorge Bergoglio, the Cardinal Archbishop of Buenos Aires, quite well. We had been made cardinals on the same day in 2001 and we had often sat next or near to each other at meetings. At the conclave of 2005 we had been part of the little group that I had jokingly named *la squadra* only because we talked a lot to each other during intervals at the conclave. I had come to know and admire Cardinal Bergoglio as a man of humility, sanity and holiness. We arranged to meet for supper to have a chat together on the Sunday evening before the first of the general congregations the following morning. Over a meal of risotto and a glass of wine we talked about the sort of person we felt the cardinals should elect. If he had any inkling at all that evening that he himself might be in the running, he gave me no indication of that possibility and nor did I raise the issue. There was a lot of talk among the cardinals of the need for someone younger, with the vigour and energy that would be needed to take on the problems and challenges that faced the Church. Bergoglio was 76 years old. I did not speak to him again until a few hours before the conclave would begin.

The general congregations began the next morning. Never before had I heard the cardinals speak so earnestly and with such openness and seriousness as I did that week. At the conclave of 2005, dominated by memories of Pope John Paul II, it seemed to me that the overriding feeling among the cardinals was that the Church was not ready for turbulence. It needed a period of continuity. In the days after the resignation of Benedict XVI, the mood was very different. Now there was a willingness to be less cautious.

Speaker after speaker, cardinals of every kind from every continent called for a reform of the governance of the Church so that it would better serve the bishops and the Church. The leaks and the financial scandals had damaged the Church's mission. There was a feeling that some of the senior officials in the curia had let the side down. If there needed to be a change at the centre, perhaps it would require someone from the outside, from the periphery, to lead it. But of course it had to be someone with energy, someone who could make things happen.

There was a very significant difference between this conclave and the 2005 conclave. Benedict's resignation itself had changed the dynamics. It began to strike me that now that we had had a resignation, the age of the pope mattered less. If the pope were to feel, after serving a number of years, that he no longer had the strength to continue, Pope Benedict had set an example. He had shown that the pope could decide to step down. So the important thing was to find the right man.

It was a busy and exciting six days for me. My feelings at this conclave were very different from 2005. I knew most of the cardinals and several of them were personal friends. If not on the first morning of our meetings, within a day or two I was becoming sure in my heart who I felt had the necessary combination of gifts to be Benedict's successor. There were certainly impressive alternatives, brilliant intellectuals and people I admired for their devotion and personal integrity. But who could be different enough and capable enough to bring about the kind of reform that was needed in the Church?

It is always unwise to think you know who 'God's candidate' is at a papal election. But I was beginning to know my mind about a man whom I thought the cardinals might choose. I remembered from the previous conclave how cardinals too old to vote had been inclined to share with their younger confreres their personal vision for the future of the Church at great length. Nevertheless, I could not resist the opportunity to speak. I reminded my brother cardinals that the word 'pontiff' comes from the Latin 'pontifex', which means 'bridge-builder'. And I felt that, more than anything, the Church needed a pope who would build bridges – with the curia, with the bishops, and with the world. Perhaps, I mused, the Vatican needed to open its gates and to let the poor of the world walk in its gardens.

The texts of the speeches made in the general congregations have not been released, but it is interesting that Pope Francis himself has often spoken of the things the cardinals had called for during these days. They had suggested that a small commission of cardinals from outside Rome be appointed to assist the new pope, whoever he would be, and they had called for a reform of the synod of bishops, and the establishment of a post-synod commission with a permanent consultative character. The cardinals had also asked for a reform of the Vatican finances and had insisted that there must be complete transparency in its dealings.

Cardinal Bergoglio was one of the last of us to speak and his intervention has since been published. I remember his speech well. He was
brief and to the point. He reminded us of who we were and what the
Church was for. 'Evangelization is the Church's reason for being', he
told us. The Church must not become wrapped up in itself; it must not
be self-referential. The Church is called to come out from itself and
to go to people on the periphery of society where there was sin, pain,
misery and injustice and to bring to them the good news of the Gospel
of Jesus Christ. If the Church does not come out of itself to evangelize,
it becomes self-referential and grows sick. 'Thinking of the next pope',
he went on, 'he must be a man who from the contemplation and
adoration of Jesus Christ helps the Church to go out to the existential
peripheries, that helps her to be the fruitful mother who gains life from
the sweet and comforting joy of evangelizing.'

Bergoglio's speech struck a new note. By the 'periphery' he did
not only mean the geographical periphery of the Catholic world, the
younger churches of sub-Saharan Africa, Asia and South America. He
was talking about the 'existential peripheries': the poor, the sick, the
old – all those pushed to the margins, the least valued and the most
vulnerable. He was also talking about the people who were on the
peripheries because they had become disenchanted with the Church,
young people for whom it had become irrelevant and people who no
longer felt welcome because for whatever reason they were unable to
participate in the fullness of its sacramental life.

There was stillness when he sat down. I looked at the faces of the
cardinals around me. Many were moved by what he said. This was the
moment, I think, when some of them began to wonder if they might
not have heard the voice of the man who would lead the Church to
recover its vigour and give it a fresh sense of direction.

On the morning the conclave was to open, all the cardinals celebrated the *Missa pro Eligenda Romana Pontifice* presided over by the senior cardinal, Angelo Sodano. As I left St Peter's after the Mass ended I found myself walking beside Cardinal Bergoglio. It was the first time we had spoken since we had shared a risotto together nine days earlier. He was on his way back to the Casa Santa Marta for lunch and a rest before the beginning of the conclave that evening. We chatted for a minute or two and as we parted my final words to him were, *'Stai attento'* ('Watch out!'). He nodded, *'Capisco'*. 'I understand', he said. He was calm. Did I know Bergoglio was going to be elected pope? No. Neither of us knew what was about to happen. Any of the men entering into the conclave might emerge as the next pope.

As at the 2005 conclave, there were 115 cardinal-electors, so the required number of votes was again 77. The cardinals had one ballot that evening, then they would continue the following day with more rounds of voting, two in the morning, two in the afternoon, until a candidate had reached the two-thirds majority. The one time I have to admit I would have loved to have been inside the 2013 conclave was on that Tuesday evening, after the first ballot, when the cardinals had walked or taken one of the buses back to the Casa Santa Marta. The first votes had been cast and the names of the leading candidates were now in their minds. Before and after supper the cardinals would sit around talking in small groups, and then one or two would move around the room from one group to another.

The following evening, Wednesday 13 March, I had arranged to offer Mass in my titular church of Santa Maria sopra Minerva. It was advertised and a large number of students and Italian parishioners attended. There would be another four ballots that day, if necessary, and my guess had been that it would take more than five ballots to decide the outcome, so I expected the conclave to last until at least Thursday. After the Gospel, I said a few words about the conclave, and urged the people there to pray for the cardinals as they made their momentous choice. Mass had started at 6 o'clock; when I came off the altar at 6.50 p.m. someone rushed up to me and said, 'White smoke! White smoke!'

It was raining when I came out of the church, but Nick Hudson, the rector of the English College, had brought his car, so we immediately got inside and drove down towards St Peter's. We didn't get far before we had to abandon the car. The news had spread, and half of Rome seemed to be walking towards St Peter's Square. How well I remember walking down the Via della Conciliazione towards St Peter's, with people on either side of me carrying umbrellas, wondering and praying about the man who soon would be coming out on the balcony and giving us his blessing. I had my own hopes in my heart, but I remember saying to myself, a sort of act of faith, 'Whoever comes out on that balcony, he will be pope and he will always have my total loyalty and support'.

When we arrived at the square, it was full of people. The rain and the lamps coming on and the people waiting and praying created a curious sensation. Nick took out his mobile phone and called Arthur Roche, who we knew would be in his office at the Congregation for Divine Worship, which had a window overlooking the square. He invited us up to join him, so a small group of us waited at his window looking over towards the central balcony of St Peter's Basilica, waiting and wondering and praying.

Finally, after about three-quarters of an hour we could see the lights coming on and the curtains twitching. I held my breath. Then the senior cardinal deacon, Jean-Louis Tauran, appeared, and we heard the familiar words, '*Annuntio vobis gaudium magnum. Habemus papam*'. We were all smiling, and there was huge cheering and waving of flags in the square below us. Who would it be? When the French cardinal announced his name, 'His Eminence Cardinal Jorge Bergoglio', there was a brief hush. Nobody had heard of this prelate from Argentina. In spite of the feverish speculation by professional Vatican-watchers, Bergoglio's name had hardly been mentioned. But then a few moments later, he came out onto the loggia and said, very simply, in Italian, '*Buona sera*'. There was an almighty cheer.

My heart leapt with joy. I just knew that this man, this new pope, would not only be different but he would be a blessing for the Church and the world. Somehow, in an instant, he immediately connected with the crowd. 'The duty of the conclave was to appoint a bishop of Rome, and it seems to me that my brother cardinals have chosen someone from the ends of the earth.' A little joke, and then that unforgettable moment when, bowing his head, he asked the people in the square to pray over him. In the extraordinary silence that followed, I gave thanks to God, knowing that in some mysterious way this man would lead the Church in a new direction and with fresh vigour.

The next day all the cardinals met the new pope one by one in the Hall of Benediction. We embraced and I assured him of my prayers. He then said: '*Dov'è la squadra?*' ('Where is the team?'). He was, of course, referring to the five cardinals who had sat in a group together at the previous conclave. He asked me to gather them together for a photograph, which I did, when all the greetings had been completed. The last thing he said to me was: 'Don't forget: give the Queen my warmest greetings.' When I got back to the English College I called the Queen's private secretary and passed on Francis's good wishes.

The formal inauguration Mass of Pope Francis took place on 19 March. The ceremony began with the new pope descending to the tomb of St Peter and praying there. Then the senior cardinal deacon bestows the *pallium* on him, and he is presented with the ring of the fisherman. I noticed it was gold-plated silver, unlike his predecessor's, which was all gold. Then six cardinals professed their obedience to him on behalf of the whole College of Cardinals. During his homily Pope Francis spoke of St Joseph, on whose feast day the Mass was celebrated. Everybody, he said, needs to care for the earth and for each other, as Joseph cared for Jesus and Mary. And he spoke of the principle that would guide his actions. 'The Pope', he said, 'when exercising power must enter ever more fully into that service which has its radiant culmination on the Cross.'

A few months later, in July, the English and Welsh bishops were together in Palazzola, outside Rome, for a retreat and we were very fortunate on the last day to have an audience with the recently elected Pope Francis. He greeted all of us very affectionately, and when he saw me, he broke into a broad smile and said: *'Tuo e colpevole!'* ('You're to blame!').

I am sure he had said the same thing to many cardinals in the previous weeks. The cardinals had certainly voted for change. But none of them expected the whirlwind that was to follow.

16

The winds of change

Pope Francis begins with people, he starts from where they are. At the very heart of Christian discipleship is the belief that Jesus Christ, in his life, death and resurrection, is present among those who follow him. Francis is very keen on dialogue with Pentecostals and other evangelical Christians, who for so long in some parts of the world have been treated as a kind of enemy of the Catholic Church. Francis is visibly relaxed and comfortable with evangelical Christians. They are, as he says, 'our brothers and sisters and fellow disciples of Jesus'.

This might be taken further. On the evening of Francis's installation I flew back to England to prepare to attend the enthronement on 21 March of the new Archbishop of Canterbury, Justin Welby, who had himself been present in Rome at the Mass Francis had celebrated to inaugurate his pontificate. It was good to be in Canterbury for that solemn occasion, remembering my own strong links and friendships with Justin's predecessors: Robert Runcie, George Carey and Rowan Williams. He now has all our support and prayers in his demanding and important role. I am sure that if Francis were to invite the leaders of all the Churches and Christian communities together, not in Rome but in some neutral place, and not with the idea of producing a document, but just to come together, for prayer and common worship, something interesting might happen.

Francis attracts people whether they are Christians or not. He reaches out to the poor and to all those on the periphery of society, because this is where we meet Jesus. As a cardinal archbishop in Buenos Aires he lived simply, cooking his own food and travelling by public transport. As pope, instead of living in the papal apartments in the Vatican he has moved into a modest suite of rooms in the Casa Santa Marta, the guest house I stayed in during the conclave of 2005. He encourages us not only to be a Church for the poor, but to be a Church of the poor. Those on the edges of the Church, even those outside it, understand that he has a word for them as well, a word of conversion, a word of looking for what is good and what is true in their lives, however broken or far from God they might imagine themselves to be.

The Church of Pope Francis will, I think, start to change a little as it begins to reflect his personal charisma and style. The second Vatican Council spoke of the College of Bishops in communion with the pope as exercising authority in the Church. In other words, a bishop, by virtue of the fact that he is a successor to the apostles of Jesus, shares decision-making in the Church with Peter. This is what is meant by 'collegiality'. This teaching is, I think, one of the great legacies of the Council. It would be difficult to argue that it has been implemented in practice. Up to now. But Francis, I think, will move this unfinished business to the top of the agenda.

The setting up within a few weeks of his election of a small group of eight, later nine, cardinals to help him in his governance of the Church and to help him plan the reform of the curia was an early sign of Francis's determination to exercise the papacy in a very different way to his predecessors. And then we saw the extraordinary synod of bishops on the family in October 2013, with Francis encouraging open and lively debate among the participants. We saw collegiality coming to life. It is not what we are used to. It is perhaps a little unsettling.

The second synod of bishops on the family in October 2015 will be an important event in the life of the Church. We are starting to see bishops preparing for it by consulting with their priests and listening to the voices of the lay people of their dioceses. The Church has become over-centralized over the centuries. We see from the history of the Church that diocesan councils and synods of local bishops, meeting to discuss and decide matters, was the usual way for the Church to govern itself up to comparatively recently. I think there is a real need to decentralize Church authority, to bring the periphery back to the centre. We must be prayerful and attentive to the Spirit of God and to the Spirit of Jesus in all the faithful, and we must be guided and taught definitively by the bishops with the pope.

It won't be easy or straightforward. It will demand patience and tough skins, but I see the best hope for us to meet the challenges that face us in the dogmatic and moral sphere to lie in 'collegiality' and in 'synodality' – and, I would add, in 'subsidiarity', because more matters involving the life of the church should be left to the local bishops to decide.

The pope has a crucial role to play in upholding unity and truth within the worldwide communion. He has to make sure that the essential teachings of the Church are upheld by his fellow bishops and that they are kept in unity with one another and with him. It seems to me that the future of the Church in Rome lies in there being no more bishops, priests, lay men and women working in the curia than are required to enable the pope fulfil this role. The curia, including the cardinals who live and work in Rome, is not there, as it were, to rule the Church with the pope. The purpose of these offices and departments

– and it is an important and valuable one – is to assist and support the bishops, always in communion with the pope, in governing and regulating the life of the Church.

I remember once, in a meeting of cardinals, suggesting that it might be better to have fewer people working in the curia: fewer cardinals and bishops, and just enough skilled and well-trained priests, lay men and women to serve the pope in his ministry. My remarks were not greeted with overwhelming enthusiasm. One cardinal said to me as we left the hall: 'So – you are trying to get rid of me?'

The winds of change are blowing through Rome. The great majority of cardinals and bishops around the world feel a sense of relief and satisfaction; a few, of course, particularly in Rome, are less happy. There is always resistance to change. I am reminded of the excitement I felt as a young curate, reading Xavier Rynne's 'Letters from the Vatican' and looking forward hungrily to the latest documents of the second Vatican Council. When I hear Pope Francis talk about going out to the peripheries, when I hear of him meeting people where they are, I think about the books of Yves Congar that inspired me as a young priest, and I think about the first small groups we started in Portsmouth and Fareham. It is often said that councils of the Church take many years to develop and bear fruit. I think that it is only now that the second Vatican Council is fully bearing the fruit that is contained in its teaching.

I must come to the end of this memoir. I am very conscious of its many inadequacies and omissions. I will be rightly chided for my failure to address many issues in greater depth. Church historians will be frustrated at the blurry factual detail and theologians may be frustrated by the lack of depth of the analysis. I have recalled how moved I was by Benedict's last address as pope. When he spoke of feeling like Peter with the other apostles in the boat on the Sea of Galilee, enjoying days when the catch had been abundant and suffering days when 'the Lord seemed to sleep', it struck a chord with me. Nevertheless, like Benedict, 'I have always known that the Lord is in the barque, and that the barque of the Church is not mine, not ours, but his – and he shall not let her sink.'

I trust in God because I know he lives in his Church which is always alive, that the Gospel's word of truth is the strength of the Church. It is often said that the Church is always reforming itself, because the Spirit of God is there in the community of believers, who welcome the grace of God in truth and live it in charity. I love it when we say at Eastertide: 'This is our faith, this is the faith of the Church and we are proud to profess it in Christ Jesus Our Lord.' I always enjoy the Mass of Chrism in Holy Week. Here the bishop is celebrating the mystery of Christ with his priests, religious and lay people. Here we have the whole mystery and gift of the Church presented in the liturgy, in the Word of God that is spoken; in the oils for the sacraments which are blessed; in the rededication of priests to their ministry, to the communion that is evident among all the faithful. It is always a most moving and holy event.

My eldest brother, Jim, died last year. He was a doctor, like George, our father. There's something of the priest about a doctor. They're there at the big moments: birth, illness, death. They're involved, yet they have to preserve a certain detachment. As a priest, you are close to the people of the parish, you live beside them, share their interests and concerns, but you can't get too involved in all the sadnesses or even all the joys. Every week, there is another tragedy, another death. Every few years, you are on the move again. It's the nature of the trade. It's a way of loving and compassion that also keeps a little distance. Jim was kind and gentle, a good man. I was glad to be here to bury him. Now I'm the last of my siblings, and it feels a little different.

A few days before I went away to the seminary at the age of 18, I went to see my parish priest in Reading, a much-revered senior priest of the diocese. I said to him: 'Canon, I am going away to Rome to study for the priesthood. Have you any advice to give me?' I was expecting something along the lines of, 'The harvest is great and you will do great work for the Church – and your mission will be an important and vital one'. I thought at least that young Murphy-O'Connor might be commended for the great sacrifice he was making. Instead, all the canon said was: 'Young man, pray for perseverance.'

I remember feeling a little deflated. I had been expecting something slightly more exciting. Yet I have always remembered the canon's words, and now as I come to the latter days of my life, I find it is perseverance that I am praying for. I am very conscious of my sins and weaknesses, my mistakes and of my many failures to be braver and more sacrificial in my life as a priest and as a bishop. Every day I ask forgiveness of God and of my brothers and sisters.

Every time I go to a funeral now, I am inclined to think that the next one will be my own. There's already a little committee planning the arrangements. I'm not quite sure what they've got in mind. Priests enjoy discussing funerals. I have a place in the cathedral earmarked for my tomb. Basil Hume and John Carmel Heenan, like Arthur Hinsley, are buried in the cathedral and not in the crypt alongside Manning, Wiseman, Griffin and Godfrey. There has been talk of doing up the chapel of St Patrick and the saints of Ireland and placing me there, but I'm not sure people go into that chapel much. I'd rather be in the nave, where people will pass by and, please God, say the occasional prayer for me.

I happened to be reading some of the prayers and meditations of John Henry Newman recently. I came across his beautiful prayer for a happy death. I would like to make it my own.

O my Lord and Saviour,

support me in that hour

in the strong arms of Thy Sacraments

and by the fresh fragrance of Thy consolations.

Let the absolving words be said over me,

and the holy oil sign and seal me,

and Thy own Body be my food and Thy blood my sprinkling;

and let my sweet Mother, Mary, breathe on me,

and my angel whisper peace to me,

and my glorious saints smile upon me;

that in them all and through them all

I may receive the gift of perseverance, and die,

as I desire to live,

in Thy faith, in Thy Church, in Thy service, and in Thy love.

Amen to that.

INDEX OF NAMES